THE CLIMA

Wole Soyinka was born on 13 July 1934, in Abeokuta, Western Nigeria, and lived with his family in the Aké quarter of the city. His homeland was then still a British dependency. His father was headmaster of an Anglican primary school, and his mother, whom he nicknamed 'Wild Christian', was a shop owner and trader. In 1981, Soyinka published *Aké*, a memoir about his youth, described in the *New York Times* as 'a classic of childhood memoirs wherever and whenever produced'.

Early on Soyinka became involved in and inspired by both Nigeria's fight for independence and the revolt in which his mother was a leading activist against a tax on women. He described the tax revolt as 'the earliest event I remember in which I was really caught up in a wave of activism and understood the principles involved. Young as I was, it all took place around me, discussions took place around me, and I knew what forces were involved. But even before [the tax revolt], I'd listened to elders talking, and I used to read the newspapers on my father's desk. This was a period of anti-colonial fervour, so the entire anti-colonial training was something I imbibed quite early, even before the women's movement.'

After studying Greek, English and History at Ibadan University in Nigeria from 1952 to 1954, Soyinka travelled to England to study English Literature at Leeds University. On graduating, he worked as a play reader for London's Royal Court Theatre, where he directed some of his own early plays. In 1960, he returned to Nigeria to research West African drama, and wrote and directed dramatic sketches critical of the government.

Four years later, Soyinka again ran foul of the government. After being accused of holding up a radio station to prevent the broadcasting of false election results, he was arrested. A protest over his imprisonment was organised by an international group of writers, including Norman Mailer and William Styron. He was acquitted after a court trial.

In 1967, at the beginning of the Nigerian civil war, he was accused of helping rebels in the breakaway republic of Biafra buy jet fighters. Soyinka was arrested but never formally charged and spent most of the next twenty-seven months in solitary confinement in a cell that measured only four feet by eight.

During his imprisonment, Soyinka surreptitiously wrote on cigarette packets, toilet paper and between the lines of books he secretly managed to acquire. Many of those scribblings were later compiled in his 1972 book *The Man Died: The Prison Notes of Wole Soyinka*.

In October 1969, Soyinka was released from prison and became chair of the Department of Theatre Arts at the University of Ibadan but the following year he went into voluntary exile in Europe for five years. During that time he served as editor of *Transition*, Africa's leading intellectual journal, and taught at the University of Ghana, Accra and Churchill College, Cambridge.

In 1975, Soyinka returned to Nigeria and the following year became professor of English at the University of Ife. During the 1970s and throughout the 1980s, he was a force in local and national politics in Nigeria and also served as a visiting professor at numerous universities, including Harvard, Yale, Cornell and Cambridge.

In 1986, Soyinka was awarded the Nobel Prize for Literature, the first African to be so honoured. The Swedish Academy described him as 'one of the finest poetical playwrights that have written in English'.

Between 1993 and 1998 Wole Soyinka was again forced into exile as a result of his opposition to a military dictatorship and its brutalities. He was tried in absentia for capital Treason, the charges being withdrawn after the fall of that government in 1998. Soyinka has since assumed a position as Professor Emeritus at Obafemi Awolowo University, Nigeria, but still teaches in universities in Europe and the USA.

(This biography is adapted from an article by John D. Thomas first published in Emory Magazine.*)*

Also by Wole Soyinka

The Open Sore of a Continent:
A personal narrative of the Nigerian Crisis

The Burden of Memory, the Muse of Forgiveness

THE CLIMATE OF FEAR

THE REITH LECTURES 2004

Wole Soyinka

PROFILE BOOKS

First published in Great Britain in 2004 by
Profile Books Ltd
58A Hatton Garden
London ECIN 8LX
www.profilebooks.co.uk

10 9 8 7 6 5 4 3 2 1

Typeset in Bembo by
MacGuru Ltd
info@macguru.org.uk
Printed and bound in Great Britain by
Bookmarque Ltd, Croydon, Surrey

A CIP catalogue record for this book is available from the British Library.

ISBN 1 86197 783 2

Contents

Preface

The first of the five-lecture series 'A changing mask of fear' took place at the Royal Institute of Science in London in March 2004. During audience intervention, I offered, in response to a question, a view that the President of the United States had deliberately exaggerated suspicions of the existence of weapons of mass destruction in Iraq. By contrast, I cautioned, it was impossible, and dangerous, for him or anyone else to underestimate the menace posed to the world by Al Queda. A voice from the audience vehemently disagreed with the second part of that comment. Yes, without question, George Bush had gone chasing shadows in Iraq, but to suggest that there was any more substance to Al Queda, a force that had been definitively routed from Afghanistan, was merely buying into a warmonger's fantasies.

Virtually the morning after that exchange, the 'corpse' of Al Queda unleashed a horrendous attack on the civilian population of Spain, littering the railway tracks of Madrid with human parts. Once again, the surprise of the event was that anyone could have been taken by surprise.

Much more has happened in that vein, not always so bloody perhaps, during those spaced-out lectures, and more has happened since. Such incidents have been merely symptomatic of the dilemma of our times. As the series continued, several events would strike me – and others also, from their comments – as unrehearsed but deadly or cautionary counterpoints of reality to the series. These include statements from world leaders, government policy decisions, self-justifications, self-reversals, military scandals, religion-inspired massacres and reprisals and so on. A number were spurts of deadly interjections from those entities that, in this series, I have described as the quasi-state. My mind could not help, for instance, but revisit the post-lecture exchanges on the theme of dignity when the scandal broke of the maltreatment, abuse and torture of Iraqi prisoners and detainees at the hands of the coalition forces. What is so often hushed up had finally entered the public domain, and with a brutal efficacy that could only shock and bewilder.

There they were, the would-be liberators, dehumanising their prisoners and evidently relishing the experience. At once the contention of power and dignity was bared – literally – in blistering images. The world was treated to the performance of power when it becomes suddenly accessible to the powerless in relation to the even more powerless: the result was a graphic demonstration of the undiscriminating arrogance of power, manifested in the humiliation – including sexual – of the weaker, those who were made so only by circumstances, not by any intrinsic qualifications, not by others' social or economic superiority – simply by circumstances that could be reversed at any moment.

Those circumstances were indeed reversed, and with an even more sickening escalation of horror, as a hostage was offered up to the world as a sacrificial lamb. The gruesome beheading of a hapless hostage in the name of reprisal, carried out in a manner that was clearly orchestrated towards global consumption, leapfrogged the incontinence of the US Army reservists in its barbarity, its arrogance and intensity of visceral laceration.

Was this killing *purely* an act of vengeance? If it were, the event would be recorded simply for periodic savouring of the wages of vengeance and/or sadistic pleasure by the perpetrators. Staged deliberately for global instruction, however, it can be read also as another statement of power, directed at the world. The quasi-state sets its own laws and strikes at will. This exhibitionist act was of a different nature from the mob fury that was unleashed on the four American contractors, the mutilated corpses of two to be later hung upside-down over a bridge in an ultimate act of desecration. That was a blood frenzy that belonged more within the psychopathology of mob susceptibility than to the statement of power. The bloody execution of a hostage, by contrast, the manner of its staging, was the communication of power, however desperate and transient.

I doubt, however, that this very act has raised the general level of fear in the mind of the average individual or, indeed, in the minds of the community. Certain acts are so far beyond the pale that they arouse the opposite emotions – anger, loathing, disgust and contempt. Contempt for the cold-blooded competitors in the stakes of human degradation.

Alas, we can hold to account only those who accept, are bound by, or can be compelled into, our code of accountability. The American forces of occupation belong within these categories; thus it is possible to express the view that they belong, like Milosevic and others, at a tribunal for crimes against humanity. If the comparative status of this crime appears not to warrant the attention of that eminent body, however, then perhaps it is time to revisit the Rome Convention and set up lower courts for crimes of lesser magnitude that none the less fall within the category of dehumanisation, although not quite on the scale of genocide or 'ethnic cleansing'. The essence of this is to make the accused – wherever and whenever – undergo a structured passage of international opprobrium, as opposed to in-house disciplinary action that only ends with the convicts selling their stories on prime time for hundreds or thousands of dollars. Already, the spectacle of the identified perpetrators strutting around their home towns, making free with American media, giving self-justifying interviews, is almost as revolting as the very crimes over which the world has risen in uproar.

Is the spiral of anti-humanism now unstoppable? If so, where will it lead? Constantly immersed in the cumulative denigration of human sensibilities, only to have one's most pessimistic predilections topped again and again by new acts – or revelations – of the limitless depth to which the human mind can sink in its negative designs, one is tempted to declare simply that the world has now entered an irreversible state of global anomie.

However, in addition to the existence on the same globe of communities that stubbornly set their course on a faith in the redemptive potential of the social being as a creature of lofty aspirations, the existence of nations and organisations that establish structures for contesting inhuman acts not merely on moral but on agreed legal principles, there are also constant reminders here and there, on both major and minor scales, of a constant striving towards the option of healing, and the establishment of just and humane communities. It is for this reason that I consider it perhaps of some value, however limited, to co-opt, as the final word of this brief preface to a rather gloomy exposition, the following excerpt from a letter I recently received in response to the lectures.

The writer was one of our contacts during the trip of a group of writers to the Middle East, referred to in the fourth lecture, 'The quest for dignity'. She wrote to inform me of the remarkable impact of the visit of the Jewish musician Daniel Barenboim to Ramallah, where he, and a newly trained orchestra of Palestinian youths, performed in concert. The resultant fervour of human belonging described in the coverage of Barenboim's presence and activities among the Palestinians evoked, for me, memories of our own visit two years earlier, one that culminated in a magical night of poetry and music that welled into the euphoria of sheer human solidarity in the ancient theatre of Ramallah.

The letter was not all, however, about that conjured space of the transcendental, when all things seem possible because of a collective immersion in an artistic experience, leading to a rare glimpse of the oneness of our universe – 'Everything is linked,' said an enraptured Barenboim on stage; 'everyone is linked, all our actions have ramifications, and music is a teacher of this inter-connected reality.' There was, however, in the letter a mundane, prosaic footnote that nibbled at the very edges of possible understanding, since understanding must always be preceded by human curiosity. Perhaps it will vanish in the charged space between one suicide bomber and the next military bulldozer that buries human beings alive within the imagined security of their own homes; perhaps it will join other shards of recollected moments of curiosity and discovery, to weld into a vessel of recep-tivity and response. No matter, here it is, and most espe-cially for the edification of that recalcitrant lobby, frozen in time, locked in negative memory, whose responses to this series sadly indicate that they cannot yet commence the journey of curiosity across a dividing wall. She writes:

> I am glad that for once I can send good news from Palestine. The enclosed articles bear witness to something beautiful, hopeful and creative that happened in Palestine last week. Reading your Reith Lecture 'The quest for dignity', I thought you would like to know about this experience. It was certainly an uplifting event and certainly an evening where the dignity and nobility of man reigned supreme. Is there a better venue than the arts to restore and inspire hope in the midst of darkness and despair?
>
> ... You might be interested to know that a relative of ours (who originally sent me your article) has sent your article to the commander in chief of the Occupation Israeli forces in our area. He had had a meeting with him yesterday and he mentioned your article and the issue of humiliation as a core factor for all that is happening etc. At the end of the meeting the general asked to see your article. So our friend sent it to him. I hope it will inspire some sense ...

To which one can only say a fervent A-men!

Wole Soyinka
May 2004

THE CLIMATE OF FEAR

1

A changing mask
of fear

I have taken myself back to the late seventies when, at the London Institute of Contemporary Arts, I delivered a lecture under the title 'Climates of art'. Introducing that lecture, I made the following admission:

> The title is, of course, deliberate. It is meant to trigger off those associative devices … so that 'Climate of fear', 'Climate of terror', and so on will surface in the mind without much conscious effort.

In the course of the lecture, variations of the title of this present series cropped up at least half a dozen times. My departure point, my main area of concern at the time, was the fate of the arts – and artists – under the burgeoning trade of dictatorship and governance through a forced diet of fear, most especially on the African continent – in common parlance, the fear of 'the midnight knock'. Arbitrary detentions. Disappearances. Torture as the rule rather than the exception. Even cynical manipulations of the judicial process, whereby a political dissident found himself in what could be described as a revolving dock without an exit, a Kafkaesque nightmare that had no end except perhaps at the end of a rope, for a crime of which the accused might even be completely unaware. Decades after that lecture, the world took bitter note of the hanging of the Nigerian activist Ken Saro-Wiwa and eight of his companions after a kangaroo trial – mostly because he was a writer, but also because his cause, that of ecological preservation, had become a global agenda.

At the time of that lecture, Nigeria, my immediate political constituency, was reeling under the execution, by firing squad, of three young men under a retroactive decree – in other words, the crime of which they were convicted, drug-trafficking, did not carry a capital forfeit at the time of commission. That defiant act of murder had a purpose – to instil fear into the populace by deliberately flouting the most elementary principles of justice. And so on and on it went. The Nigerian event wrung two plays out of me – *A Scourge of Hyacinths* for radio, and *From Zia with Love*, its stage version – so persistently did that episode insist on lacerating my re-creative temper. I was not alone. The entire nation was deeply traumatised. Even the normally carnivalesque atmosphere that marked the main arena of public executions of armed robbers, dubbed the Bar Beach Show, was reported unusually subdued. So improbable was the outcome that the crowd had persuaded itself to believe a rumour that the military dictatorship intended only to mount a charade, instil some salutary fear into traffickers, and would reprieve the young men at the last moment. Instead of giving voice to the usual chorus of derision at the exit of hated felons, the crowd had come prepared to cheer the moment of reprieve. When the ritual of final priestly ministrations, blindfolding and other motions made it quite clear that the sentence was moving remorselessly towards its decreed end, a shout of 'No, no, no' went up among the crowd. After the deed was done, there followed moments of absolute silence, of utter disbelief; then the crowd more or less slunk away, downcast and shocked. The dictators had not expected such a reaction. Not long after, public executions were banned and, following the overthrow of that dictatorship by another, the edict was repealed.

While that regime lasted, however, there was no question about it: for the first time in the brief history of her independence, the Nigerian nation, near uniformly, was inducted into a palpable intimacy with fear. The question on every mind was simply this: what else were they capable of, those who could carry out an act that revolted even the most elastic sectors of the public conscience? It is a question to bear in mind in our attempts to understand what distinguishes, from the past, the new fabric of fear that we all seem to wear at this moment. As each assault on our localised or global sense of security is mounted or uncovered in the nick of time, the residual question is surely: What next? Where? How? Are limits or restraints any longer recognised?

What was happening on the African continent in those violent seventies and eighties was echoed, perhaps with even greater ferocity, in the Americas, where those danger words *desaparecidos, right-wing murder squads, government-sponsored vigilantes, etc.* – gained international notoriety. Nicaragua, Chile, Argentina, Panama. Iran under the SAVAK. Apartheid South Africa under BOSS. Fear was near uniformly a state-run production line, except of course where right-wing volunteer agents of repression lent a hand – in Latin America especially. Between right-wing governments and the efficient state-run communist machinery there was, however, hardly any difference. Hungary, Albania, East Germany, Bulgaria and so on. Émigrés from these would-be utopias, no different from survivors of apartheid South Africa – both the defeated and the yet combative and conspiratorial – criss-crossed the world seeking help and solidarity. Again and again, our paths – those of creative people – would meet, leading to that

4

immediate question: how did creativity survive under such arbitrary exercise of power? How did Art survive in a climate of fear? Today, the constituency of fear has become much broader, far less selective.

We are all agreed, I like to believe, on what constitutes fear. If not, we can at least agree on the symptoms of fear, recognise when the conditioning of fear has afflicted or been imposed on an individual or a community. Certainly we have learnt to associate the emotion of fear with the ascertainable measure of a loss in accustomed volition. The sense of freedom that is enjoyed or, more accurately, taken for granted in normal life, becomes acutely contracted. Caution and calculation replace a norm of spontaneity or routine. Often, normal speech is reduced to a whisper, even within the intimacy of the home. Choices become limited. One is more guarded, less impulsive. A rapist is on the loose in society. A serial killer terrorises an entire community – as happened recently in the state of Maryland in the United States, where two men, an adult and his protégé, placed an entire state under siege as they picked off victims at random.

Now, such a disruption induces a totally different sensation from that created by a war situation, where a town is placed under siege. Even if bombs and rockets are raining down on the populace without cessation, the very process of war permits a certain space of volition, and thus reduces the inner debilitation that comes with a sense of impotence. In the case of Maryland, the murdering pair succeeded in making fear the controlling factor for a population. This anonymous force shut down schools and institutions and destabilised normal existence. Parents took to escorting their children right into the schoolroom, with a look cast over the shoulder. Obviously, while the killing spree lasted, there was deep resentment of, even rage at, the unknown assailant, but the commonest product of that phase was simply undirected fear. A notable aspect of all-pervasive fear is that it induces a degree of loss of self-apprehension: a part of one's self has been appropriated, a level of consciousness, and this may even lead to a reduction in one's self-esteem – in short, a loss of inner dignity. Not always, admittedly, and those times when such a claim is invalid offer us the chance of making some crucial distinctions among the various contexts within which fear takes its especial quality.

It so happens that I recently underwent an experience that enables me to reinforce such a distinction, one that may explain why the experience of fear is actually more tolerable in some circumstances than in others – in other words, there does exist a kind of fear one can live with, shrug off, one that may actually be absorbed as a therapeutic incidence, while others are simply downright degrading. I refer to the recent fires that ravaged southern California and resulted in the devastation of a larger swathe of land, we are told, than ever in the history of fires in the United States. I was one of those thousands of residents who found their homes in the path of the ravenous invader, unable to predict – literally – which way the wind would blow.

Well, let me describe what I observed in the comportment of neighbours. They were anxious, of course, and fearful. Watchful and insecure. But their humanity was not abused or degraded by the menace that bore down on them. On the contrary, they remained in combative form, constantly exchanging news as well as tactical suggestions for saving the neighbourhood. Sleep was out of the question. At any moment, we had been warned, police sirens and fire-truck klaxons could rip through the night, signalling the moment for compulsory evacuation. As the fires came closer, choices became reduced. Sprinklers lost power, garden hoses gave up the last trickle, and we began to wonder if electric power was now threatened. Indeed, a blackout soon followed. Our endangered community became apprehensive of the worst – but no one was truly intimidated, nor was there the slightest sign of a loss of dignity.

The relationship between that fire, a naked force of Nature – even though probably the work of arsonists – and the humanity that was menaced was very different from the exercise of the power of an individual over another, or that of a totalitarian state over its populace. There exists a vast abyss of sensibilities between the raw force that is Nature, on the one hand, and the exertion of force by one human being in relation to another. I suggest that this has to do with yet another human possession, an attribute that is as much a social acquisition as it is inherent in the human species – dignity. A number of philosophers – Hegel, Locke and so on – even stretch this notion of self-esteem to the human need for *recognition*. This last is a concept of which I am not particularly enamoured, and I find the bulk of expository literature on that extended impulse mostly unsatisfying – we shall touch again on this theme in our fourth lecture, 'The quest for dignity'. For now, let us simply observe that the assault on human dignity is one of the prime goals of the visitation of fear, a prelude to the domination of the mind and the triumph of power.

A few decades ago, the existence of collective fear had an immediately identifiable face – the atomic bomb. While that source is not totally absent today, one can claim that we have moved beyond the fear of the bomb. A nuclear menace is also implicated in the current climate of fear, but the atom bomb is only another weapon in its arsenal, the theoretical do-it-yourself kit that fits into a suitcase and can be assembled in the nearest toilet. What terrifies the world, however, is no longer the possibility of over-muscled states unleashing on the world the ultimate scenario – the *Mutual Assured Destruction* (MAD) that once, paradoxically, also served as its own mutually restraining mechanism. Today the fear is one of furtive, invisible power, the power of the quasi-state, that entity that lays no claim to any physical boundaries, flies no national flag, is unlisted in any international associations, and is every bit as mad as the MAD gospel of annihilation that was so calmly annunciated by the superpowers.

The last century, post-Second World War, was indeed dominated by the fear of a nuclear holocaust. That fear, let it be noted, however, was only a successor to another. It replaced, once the war was over, yet another collective fear – that of world domination by a fanatic individual who preached, and sought to actualise, a gospel of race purity. In the cause of that mission, some millions of humanity were systematically annihilated, while millions more perished on fields of battle that stretched from the North Pole to the South Sea Islands. As I narrated in my childhood memoirs, *AKE: The Years of Childhood*, the figure of Adolf Hitler was one fearsome presence that percolated distances, all the way from embattled Europe to far-flung colonial possessions. Parents invoked Hitler as the bogeyman to quiet the obstreperous child. Households were compelled by decree of the colonial officer to darken their windows at night. Infractions were penalised by fines. And when, finally, a cargo ship caught fire on the lagoon in the capital city of Lagos, and explosions shattered windows even far away from the Marina, we, as children, had no doubt that the Terror of the Free World had indeed arrived to cart us off into slavery.

That universal season of fear ended on the battlefield. In its place rose the fear of the very weapon of the world's liberation – at least, that was the excuse – whose devastating effects appeared to have no limitations. The literature of science fiction took a swing towards prospects of a devastated world, peopled by mutants in whom the loss of the last vestiges of humanity would be reflected in their very physical decomposition. The cinema bore graphic witness to this mood. Beyond the grotesquerie, the caricatures and the gallows humour of *Dr Strangelove* was a more than subterranean revelation of a penetrating fear, a caution and a strong moral message to the world to pull back from the nuclear brink. Nothing was left to chance in its aim of exacting a moral apprehension of power and destruction through a recourse to negative memory – who can forget Peter Sellers's manic performance, the arm that jerked up of its own volition in a Nazi salute, an iconography that was surpassed only by the whooping, rodeo ride on the back of a nuclear bomb into oblivion and obliteration by yet another obsessed angel of MAD!

That fear went, predictably, beyond artistic expressions and provoked practical responses. There were protest marches, Aldermaston being perhaps the pioneer and the most famous of them all. I took part in some of these, enjoyed their carnival atmosphere that was laced with purpose. I was filled with excitement at participating in what struck me as a pre-emptive course of action by civil society. I felt that I was part of a universal undertaking – not to mention the thrill of actually marching in the company of the British philosopher Bertrand Russell, incidentally the first Reith lecturer in 1948. My fond recollection of him remains that of a pipe-smoking leprechaun of a man with a giant brain, whose atheism was grounded in a faith that man's first allegiance was to his kind, and that science must always be subject to humanistic considerations.

As the sabre-rattling grew louder during this Cold War, and the superpowers raced to surpass one another in mounting bigger and better explosions, sneak a few of the deadly pods into the backyards of their ideological rivals, the fear of the atom bomb grew so affective that a few of my European acquaintances chose not to have any children, declaring that they were not about to provide fodder for the inevitable nuclear consummation. Some formed artist colonies on remote islands where they established communes, leading a simple life, culturing seaweed – for some reason that I cannot now recall – while they awaited the inevitable, from which, however, they fully expected to be spared. Folk singers, such as Pete Seeger, became cult figures on international circuits for their anti-nuclear lyrics. Tom Lehrer's songs, laced with grim, apocalyptic humour, became staple diet for student and anti-establishment caucuses, while the great baritone Paul Robeson lent credence to a great communist conspiracy by his appearances at socialist peace rallies in France, where the anti-nuclear theme overwhelmed virtually every other global concern.

Within my own continent, however, it would have been virtually impossible to find one extreme example of the pre-emptive strategies that were adopted by the artist colonies of Europe, not even when the French rode rough-shod over the protestations of African nations and detonated the first nuclear device on African soil in the middle of the last century. Africans were already inured to other forms of fear, and a nuclear conflagration was such an exotic threat that the French explosion remained a pure political aggravation, not one that ever translated into a visceral fear. Today, few of us on the continent will deny that the circumstances, and the dimension, of the current face of fear have transformed awareness even in our normally immune corners of the globe and brought into immediacy the charms of Europe's artistic exodus. The only trouble is, such overactive imaginations will find it difficult to think of a secure destination. Events of a hitherto unimaginable dimension have rendered virtually every corner of the globe vulnerable.

Reality is indeed catching up with science fiction, or, shall we now simply say, history is repeating itself in a phenomenon that appears to have been cloned from fiction. I refer to that perennial motif of the literature of megalomania, a fascination with the notion of one individual's obsession to dominate the world – to be distinguished from ruling, or governing, simply to *dominate* – that stuff of science fiction that found reality in the historic aberration of an Adolf Hitler. Now James Bond 007 moves beyond the fantasy derring-dos where the global sword of Damocles is an orbiting satellite, awaiting the push of a button unless a hundred billion euros are paid into a special account and the whole world acknowledges a new Master of the Universe, ensconced in the bowels of some inaccessible island. However, even the orbiting pod of destruction has its limitations in instilling universal fear. Far more effective is the domesticated agency whose very ordinariness is more terrifying than the sophisticated bomb, and is inversely proportionate to the bomb's lethal reach. A sachet of sarin is located no one knows where, but is ready to be punctured when the signal is given. The banal shopping bag left innocuously at the entrance to a metro station is eyed as a potential enemy, capable of devastation less dramatic than, but every bit as awesome as, a plane hurtling down from the sky in a ball of flames.

~

In 1989, a few months after the year of Lockerbie, a UTA passenger flight – UTA, like PanAm, has since collapsed – was brought down by an act of sabotage over the Republic of Niger. That event was swallowed with total equanimity by African heads of state. Was this from policy, the tranquillising pill of African and/or Third World solidarity, that catechism of historic victims of European imperialism that urged them to close ranks in the face of any accusations by the historic oppressors of the world? Or did this muteness emanate from fear of probable reprisal by the aggressor who was predictably intolerant of any voice – within or without – that dared to criticise its methods of anti-imperialist challenge?

That silence, I confess, gave me pause, and here is why. In the original lecture to which I referred at the beginning – 'Climates of Art' – when French arrogance sought to spread the fear of the nuclear holocaust on to African soil, even during that immediate post-independence stage of insecure nationhood, I lauded the fact that African states had not hesitated to act in concert. The outrage of a continent was vocal and sustained. France was declared a pariah nation, and numerous African countries broke diplomatic relations with the arrogant Gauls for infesting African soil with nuclear fumes. The economic consequences, in the main, were bravely ignored. On a personal level, since that outrage coincided with my début on the stage of the Royal Court Theatre in London – one of those experimental one-night stands on a Sunday – I declaimed an angry poem in condemnation of such an act of continental disdain. Indeed, the recent hysterical mood of resentment in the United States over the refusal of France to jump into an unnecessary US-promoted war with Iraq was nothing compared with the mood of the African continent when France, despite stern warnings, went ahead and detonated its atom bomb. With that concerted response on my mind, I think I could be forgiven for expecting no less than the same heated reaction when a plane was deliberately blasted out of African skies.

Nothing of the sort took place. A planeload of humanity had been deliberately blown apart and, suddenly, the political touchiness of the continent appeared to have gone to sleep. None of that earlier fervour of moral outrage was forthcoming, not even a credible warning to whomever the perpetrators were to kindly take their warfare elsewhere or be confronted with the righteous anger of African nations. The commencing view on the continent was that this was a PLO gambit, aided and abetted by some Middle East allies, and there were sufficient reasons to lean towards such a view. Libya – and Gaddafi – entered the list of suspects some time later.

That studied muteness, I felt, could only be born out of fear. The political club that was then the Organisation of African Unity made only the most tepid statements of condemnation. If it set up its own technical commission of investigation, it must have been deliberately low-key, an apologetic step that was shrouded in mystery – for fear of reprisals? Political cowardice or a lack of moral will, what dominated the thinking of many African leaders was, frankly, 'Let us keep mute and maybe he will exempt us from his current revolutionary rampage, or at least exercise his restraining influence and cloak us in selective immunity.' They had only to recall that Libya, headed by a young maverick called Gaddafi, was then at the height of its powers. It advertised a progressive, even radical, agenda, one that threatened corrupt as well as repressive governments, provided a training ground for dissidents of the left, right or indeterminate – and not merely on the African continent. In short, the fear of Libya was the beginning of wisdom.

That silence obtained its rebuke when contrasted with the combative cry of the world over Lockerbie. It was indeed a shock of contrasts. In the case of Lockerbie, a painstaking exercise of detective work spanned continents. The culprits were not only identified but boldly advertised, and a pursuit of the malefactors undertaken until they were eventually brought before a court of justice. That culture of 'neighbourly reticence' – let us take note – is yet again paralysing the will of African leaders today as they turn a blind eye to the genocidal operations currently being waged in the Sudan. A new Rwanda is in the making – to cite the belated acknowledgement by the Secretary-General of the United Nations – but the victims wait in vain for the moral outcry of a continent, or a structure of relief from the global community.

Again, an updated postscript to the pairing of those

two aerial assaults: in the terms of settlements finally agreed in the last year by the Libyan government, the Niger atrocity appeared to be constantly attached as a footnote, a minor codicil to the Lockerbie agreement, almost an afterthought. Those terms of settlement, being derisory in comparison, further bore out my earlier plaint: even in the supposedly egalitarian domain of death, some continue to die more equally than others. But the succession of Lockerbie by Niger had at least impressed one fact on the world: the enthronement of a qualitatively different climate of fear, an expression of global dominance through a disregard for innocents, without respect to territory, and without even a pragmatic questioning of the possible rupturing of existing political alliances. Libya was after all – still is – a member of the Organisation of African Unity, now the Africa Union. That fact did not prevent her assault on the constituency of that organisation. The implicit proclamation appeared to be that, in the new arena of conflicts, there would be no cordon sanitaire, no sanctuary for innocents, no space that was out of bounds in the territorial claims of a widening climate of fear.

Even as the foregoing was being drafted, just a few months ago, the world was astounded by a once unthinkable volte-face by the Libyan government. I listened in a state of near-hypnosis as the Libyan leader stepped up to the microphones to renounce not only the manufacture of weapons of mass destruction but –

terrorism! Within the radical caucuses of the sixties, seventies and eighties on the African continent, any suggestion that Mr Gaddafi was remotely linked with the promotion of acts that involved the arbitrary disposition of lives, and should be condemned for this, was greeted with those *knowing* smirks that declared one a victim of Western brainwashing and an enemy of the anti-imperialist struggle. The notion that there should be rules and restraints even within an accepted mandate of justifiable violence in the cause of a people's liberation was simply too abstruse a concept, one that identified only the lackeys of the imperialist order. Distasteful though the conclusion may be to such mind-sets, September 11, 2001 has proved to be only a culmination of the posted signs that had been boldly scrawled on the sands of the Sahara, over decades, in letters of blood.

We are repeatedly bombarded with the notion that the world we once knew ended on September 11, 2001. I find myself unable to empathise with such a notion, and we shall look at the reasons why as we proceed with our series. For now, let me simply admit that it is within that subjective context that I found it most appropriately symbolic that I, the only African passenger aboard a British Airways flight between London and Los Angeles on that day, should be the last person on the plane to learn what had happened, and perhaps one of the last million or two of the world population to know that the world had, allegedly, undergone a permanent transformation. It is an appropriate anecdote on which to end this introductory lecture.

What happened was quite simple: my routine on an aircraft – which I regret to admit has virtually become my third or fourth home – is quite simple. I take advantage of the total isolation to do some work, eat at mealtimes, doze off in fits and starts, drink any amount of wine I feel like – in defiance of medical wisdom – but mostly engage in a sometimes intensive dialogue with my laptop. On September 11, the routine was no different. I must have been in one of my sleep modes when the event occurred. When I woke up, I simply reported back for duty with my laptop.

My surprise was quite subdued when, eight to nine hours after take-off, I heard the pilot announce that we were now approaching Manchester – a subdued surprise because the United States makes free with the names of cities from all over the world, and I imagined that the weather had forced the pilot to follow a different flight pattern from the norm, one that brought him over some American town called Manchester, rather than the city of Boise, Idaho, a name I had grown accustomed to hearing from the flight deck as we drew close to Los Angeles. However, when, a few minutes later, the same voice announced that we were now crossing the Welsh border, I had to wonder if this was not one coincidence too many. Before I had time to work out what it all meant, however, the next announcement informed me that we were making our approach for a landing in ... Cardiff! I pressed the bell and the flight steward came by. Why, I asked, were we landing in Cardiff, and could he inform me in what part of the United States that was situated?

The poor man blinked hard, stared down at me. Didn't I know that we had turned around in mid-Atlantic? There had been, he said, a 'security incident' in the United States and all planes were being either diverted or not permitted to take off at all if their destination was the US. We were headed for Cardiff because there were no more berths at Heathrow, other US-bound planes having been grounded. Beyond that, he could offer no explanation. I shrugged it off. It was not, after all, the first time that my plane had been diverted or done a full turnaround, mid-Atlantic, on account of some technical problem.

Here is an appropriate moment to confess to my own five-year cohabitation with a personalised form of fear. Nothing less than fear had long since schooled me into travelling with only hand luggage. I have always been a light traveller, but the habit became *de rigueur* under the terror reign of Sanni Abacha of Nigeria. So unscrupulous were the methods of that dictatorship that its agents did not hesitate to introduce contraband, specifically hard drugs, into the luggage of the opposition, then alert the customs officials at the destination of the approaching drug baron. If I lived under any real fear during the struggle to rid the nation of that dictatorship, it was definitely that, over and above anything else. It surpassed even the possibility of being seduced by a designing female, like the hapless whistle-blower on the Israeli nuclear activities whose pleasure cruise with his paramour ended up in the net spun by the Mossad, and a life sentence. Against such a predicament one could at least protect oneself by resisting temptation; checked-in luggage was far more vulnerable matter. This project of incrimination through baggage-tampering actually succeeded with a traditional monarch who had refused to surrender his domain to Abacha's campaign for a life presidency. I was involved in what were fortunately successful efforts to extricate that innocent from a virtual illegal imprisonment in London, public embarrassment and even extortion.

The fear of Abacha had thus turned me into one baggageless passenger you could swear by on any flight, and thus the very first out of the customs area – that is, when I was not being interrogated for having three passports stuck together, covered with visas and immigration stamps from cover to cover. This time, passage was smooth. I ensconced myself in the bus that had been provided to take us to our hotel, settled down with a book. An hour, one and a half, then nearly two hours later, I was still seated in the bus, increasingly impatient, joined by only a handful of fellow passengers. Cardiff was apparently not accustomed to receiving so many jumbo jets all at once, and the baggage-handlers were in a total flounder.

I got down to look for someone at whom to rail for the delay, stretch my legs, find out into what hotel we were booked and look for a taxi – then recognised some of the passengers huddled around a mobile telephone, while others queued up for the public equipment. Only then did I begin to suspect that something truly out of the ordinary was responsible for our turnaround. I approached the mobile-telephone owner who was transmitting to his circle live developments from the United States. That was how, nine to ten hours after the event, I came to know that the world I knew was supposed to have disappeared, or become altered unrecognisably.

Well, I must confess that the world still looked the same to me, not only on the outside but from what I sensed inside. And this was because my mind flashed in that instant to the day, twelve years earlier, when, for me, the world chose to pretend that nothing unusual had occurred over the continent of Africa, at the edge of the Sahara, knowing full well that agents of a yet unidentified cause had sown the seeds of fear in the hearts of millions of people. The leadership of the world, including the leadership of that continent, chose to absorb this abnormality as only yet another incident in the war of causes, though even the most tenuous rules of engagement had been unilaterally rewritten to eradicate the rights of the innocent.

What had I expected? I suppose an equivalent at least of the sense of universal outrage that greeted the destruction of the World Trade Center, an event timed deliberately to take the maximum toll of innocents. Nineteen eighty-nine for me was, therefore, the moment when the world first appeared to have stood still, waiting for a response whose commensurate nature was required to restart the motions of the globe. That response was lacking, at least in intensity, certainly in its neglect of a global repudiation, and mobilisation. That lack consecrated Lockerbie, paved the way for Air India years later – a contribution that was attributed to Hindu extremists – and set the scene for September 11, 2001. From Niger to Manhattan, the trail of fear had stretched and broadened to engulf the globe, warning its inhabitants that there were no longer any categories of the involved or non-involved. No longer could not just innocents, but even a community of historic victims who inhabit the African continent, lay claim to a protective immunity.

Just as there has been gloating on that continent over the predicament of white settler farmers in Zimbabwe, and a history of colonial injustice is held by some to justify current injustices even against former victims of that same injustice, while a suffocating climate of fear envelops the entire land and its citizens, black and white, even so was there gloating in places, including open festivities, over September 11, as the world was sentenced to life imprisonment behind the bars of fear. And the judges? Are they identified and/or justified by history? By geography? Race? Ideology? Or religion? That emotive last especially, religion – and, unquestionably, the occupation of world centre stage by Islam during this epoch of global fear is a phenomenon that has provoked extreme reactions, from the attribution of collective responsibility on the one hand, to the guilt-ridden avoidance language of political correctness on the other. We shall explore some of these viewpoints in succeeding lectures.

Let it suffice for now to acknowledge that responses to any challenge to the security of human society and, indeed, survival are bound to be varied, some shaped by the history of unjust global relationships, others by instinctive partisanship – ideological, religious, racial and so on – in a world that has become truly polarised. Any course of action, or inaction, that appears to encourage impunity implicates, however, the submission of the world to a regimen of fear. Yet that very recognition makes it possible to propose that it is within collective, not unilateral, action – a theme to which we shall return in this series – that we can sustain the hopes of humanity's survival. Terror against terror may be emotionally satisfying in the immediate, but who really wants to live under the permanent shadow of a new variant of the world's ... Mutual Assured Destruction?

2

Of power and
freedom

The totalitarian state is easy to define, easy to identify, and thus offers a recognisable target at which the archers of human freedom can direct their darts. Not so obliging is what I have referred to as the quasi-state, that elusive entity that may cover the full gamut of ideologies and religions, contends for power but is not defined by physical boundaries that identify the sovereign state. Especially frustrating is the fact that the quasi-state often commences with a position whose basic aim – a challenge to an unjust status quo – makes it difficult to separate from progressive movements of dissent, with which, too, it sometimes forms alliances of common purpose. At the same time, however, there lurks within its social intent an equally deep contempt for those virtues that constitute the goals of other lovers of freedom. Thus, to grasp fully the essence of power, we must look beyond the open 'show of force', the demonstration of overt power whose purpose is to instruct a people just who is master. We are obliged to include – indeed, to regard as an equal partner in the project of power – the elusive entity that is conveniently described here as the quasi-state. We shall return to that mimic but potent entity in a few moments.

The formal state, in its dictatorial or belligerent mutation, represents power at its crudest – African nations, caught in an unending spiral of dictatorships and civil wars, are only too familiar with this exegesis of power. Equally familiar, to many, are the daylight or night-time shock troops of state, storming the homes and offices of dissidents of a political order, carting away their victims in total contempt of open or hidden resent-ment. The saturation of society by near-invisible secret agents, the co-option of friends and family members – as has been notoriously documented in Ethiopia of the Dergue, former East Germany, Idi Amin's Uganda, among others, all compelled to report on the tiniest nuances of discontent with, or indifference towards, the state – these constitute part of the overt, structured forces of subjugation. To apprehend fully the neutrality of the power of fear in recent times, indifferent to either religious or ideological base, one need only compare the testimonies of Ethiopian victims under the atheistic order of Mariam Mengistu with those that emerged from the theocratic bastion of Iran under the purification orgy of her religious leaders. The Taliban remains a lacerating memory of anti-humanism, as does the Stalinist terror in the former Soviet Union.

Gruesome as we may find the histories of formal dictatorships both of the left and of the right, however, it is to be doubted that the fear engendered by such regimes ever succeeded in percolating through to a visceral level as the totally unpredictable state-in-waiting, one that repudiates even the minimal codes of accountability that are, admittedly, often breached by the formal states. It is these that constitute the quasi-states, often meticulously structured but shadowy corporations of power that mimic the formal state in all respects except three: the already noted lack of boundaries, the lack of government secretariats with identifiable ministries and, by extension, the responsibility of governance. The quasi-state, complete with a hierarchy of élites and its own monitoring – i.e. policing and enforcement – agencies, may indeed look to a future world order but, in the process, humanity is blatantly declared expendable, and the actualisation of that new order is limited to a close cabal, proliferating through warrens and cities, and contemptuous of boundaries.

Stalin's Soviet Union is gone. Afghanistan of the Taliban is no more. It is the quasi-state that today instils the greatest fear, a condition that becomes almost neurotic where the real state, through its renegade choices, also conducts its affairs through the cultivation of the quasi-state, and thus in effect has its cake and eats it. Allied with an agency of terror that derives from its formal powers and enjoys its connivance, it sports, Janus-like, two faces, denying its furtive ally any formal recognition, but empowering it as the same time. This was a common strategy during the Cold War, when one axis created its own secretive terror machine, launched it as a virtually autonomous arm of state policy, but studiously cultivated a distancing from its existence and operations. A poison-tipped umbrella carries out its mission on a dissident in the streets of London, all the way from its origination in the Soviet Bloc. The death squads of a right-wing dictatorship from Latin America reach out and blow up a haunt or offices of dissident intellectuals in Spain or Lisbon. A state deploys a relay of suicide bombers well beyond its borders. The 'leader of the free world', the United States, explores the project of assassinating the leader of an ideological enemy and irritant through a detonating cigar. A Pope comes close to premature beatification from the tortuous foreign policies of a rabid member of an ideological bloc. A planeload of innocents is taken out in mid-air with state connivance. So much for the hybrid entity.

On its own, however, the resistance manifesto of the quasi-state can prove seductive. Only rarely does it make the mistake of showing its hand in advance, as happened in Algeria. In that nation, decades of neglect, state corruption and alienation of the ruling élite swung the disenchanted populace at the democratic elections of 1992 towards a radical movement, the electorate remaining more or less indifferent to the fact that the change threatened to place a theocratic lid on many of the secular liberties that they had learnt to take for granted. Bread and shelter are more pressing issues, in the immediate, than notions of freedom of taste. Thus: *we shall ascend to power on the democratic ladder* – declared the evidently popular Islamist party – *after which we shall pull up the ladder, and there shall be no more democracy.* Let us spend a little time on the Algerian scenario; it holds many lessons for us and, of course, occupies the tragic role of being one of the unwitting dispersal agencies of human resources for our ongoing climate of fear.

Algeria is merely a convenient example, but it is also a subjective choice for me, I am compelled to admit. My generation grew up under the indirect education of a singularly vicious anti-colonial struggle – the Algerian – one that surpassed in its intensity even that of the Kenyan Mau Mau-led nationalist revolt. That struggle easily qualifies as the most brutal of Africa's wars of liberation right up to the independence decade of the continent – the nineteen sixties. In addition, Algeria played a key role in the formation of the radical corps of African – and even black American – nationalism in the fifties and sixties, served as a source of reference, solidarity and material aid for many African revolutionary leaders from Guinea and Ghana to the Congo and South Africa. This North African country belonged in the radical sector of African nations that eventually closed ranks with the more conservative group for the formation of the Organisation of African Unity. Given such a history, it is perhaps inevitable that my generation would take more than a passing interest in the contemporary fortunes of that nation. As a newly independent entity, its experiments in post-colonial reconstruction provided study models in the quest for the developmental transformation of other newly independent African nations.

To watch such a people plunged into a state of social retrogression, from whatever cause, is a harrowing cautionary tale, truly tragic, a reminder of the Sisyphean burden that unforeseen forces often place on the shoulders of would-be progressive movements. It is a daily reminder never to take any political situation for granted, never to underestimate the focused energy of the quasi-state whose instinctive recourse to the rule of fear as a weapon of struggle drives the best minds of a nation into exile, liquidates others, and paralyses the creative drive of a dynamic people.

Algeria, in 1992, was a dilemma posed to try the credentials of the hardiest democrat anywhere in the world but, most pertinently, her African co-habitants across the Sahara, who, in many cases, were then struggling to free themselves from the stranglehold of military dictatorship. That dilemma can be summed up thus: *if you believe in democracy, are you not thereby obliged to accept, without discrimination, the fall-outs that come with a democratic choice, even if this means the termination of the democratic process itself?* This was the crux of the electoral choice that was freely made by the Algerian people. Why indeed should a people not, in effect, redeem Hegel from Karl Marx? They would only be paying Marx back in his own coin, since Marx's boast was that he began with the model of Hegel's schema of history but then turned Hegel on his head. He replaced Hegel's idealism with a materialist basis and the class struggle. Both are agreed on the dialectical process that leads to the fulfilment of history in the emasculation of the state order. Social contradictions are resolved and political strife is eliminated. Rulership becomes indistinct from followership – in one case, through the benevolent embodiment of enlightened rule, in the other, through the eradication of classes.

What the Islamic Party of Algeria did was simply to embody the historic will, or spirit, in the Koran. Ironically, this ought to be regarded as a democratic advance on Hegel, since the process of this annulment of history was reached through popular choice, and the mantle of interpreters of the historic will – summed up by Fukuyama as 'The End of History' – has been bestowed on the theocratic class by the electorate itself. Who can argue against the proposition that choice remains the bedrock of the democratic process, and if a people have made a choice that eliminates all further necessity for the ritual rounds of choosing, well ... that argument appears to have reached its terminal point. History has been fulfilled.

The problem with that argument, of course, is that this denies the dynamic nature of human society, and preaches that the purely fortuitous can substitute, at any time, for the eternal and immutable. Such a position opens the way for the triumph of a social order that is based on the concept of the Chosen – a mockery of the principle of choice if ever there was one! – and totally eliminates the impulse to change as a factor of human development. On the political field, it entrusts power permanently in the hands of a clique of rulers whose qualification could rightly range from membership of a military class to that of a Masonic order, or a labour or scientific union where specific circumstances have placed such a body in a position to resolve an over-whelming catastrophe or even dilemma. Wherever history is conceded its hour of fulfilment, revelation replaces enquiry or experiment, dictation replaces debate. For us in Nigeria in 1992, these were no abstract issues, much as we wished Algeria would simply go away or choose another time to pose a dilemma that provided ammunition for our own stubborn dictatorial order.

Let us quickly recapitulate, for those to whom both Nigeria and Algeria belong on an alien planet – or, as in some encounters I have had, are indeed the same nation since they sound alike. What happened was that in both countries – in 1992 in one case, 1993 in the other – a recognised political party looked all set to win an election. At that point, however, the process was truncated by the military for no other reason than that it did not like the face of the winners. There was a critical difference, however. The victorious party in Nigeria did not promote a manifesto that would abrogate all further democratic ventures, while in the Algerian case this formed the core of its manifesto. You will understand therefore why, whenever anyone approached me for an opinion on the situation in Algeria after those elections, I quickly looked for an escape route. Easy enough to simplify the issue and say, yes, take the democratic walk to its logical conclusion, but then, as we have attempted to question, just what is the logical conclusion of the democratic option? Dictatorship of a kind different from the dictatorial status quo?

Perhaps we can approach this dilemma obliquely, citing a very recent, and instructive, development within Nigeria – one that is, however, only a partial and tepid echo of the Algerian situation. Following the May 2003 elections, the second since that nation's return to democracy, a state in the north, Zamfara – progressively followed by nine others in the nation – declared that its governance would henceforth be based on the Sharia – a code of strict Islamic laws. One of the later subscribers to Sharia rule was the Taraba State. In December that same year, the governor, himself a Muslim, found himself obliged to take stern measures against an extremist movement that named itself after the Taliban. This group rose against the state government, claiming that it had failed to keep strict adherence to the Sharia. The sect launched an insurrection, took over some police stations – one of which, incidentally, it renamed Afghanistan – inflicted a number of casualties and sought to overthrow the elected government. It was subdued by state forces, the movement banned and the Council of Ulammas, the religious leaders, dissolved.

Would it be totally illogical to project that this could also easily have been the fate of Algeria if indeed the victorious party had succeeded in forming a government? Once righteousness replaces rights in the exercise of power, the way is paved for a permanent contest based on the primacy of the *holier-than-thou*.

However, this is mere speculation. What we do know, as fact, is that since the undemocratic choice was made in Algeria, over 150,000 lives have been lost, several of these in a most grisly manner. And not just writers, cinéastes, painters, journalists, intellectuals – those purveyors of impure thoughts who are always the primary targets of fundamentalist reformers and thinkers – though these, as usual, have also been at the forefront of carnage. We are speaking here of entire villages and sectors of urban society that were considered guilty of flouting, at some level or the other, the purist laws of the opposition, now transformed into a quasi-state, or simply of failing to show sufficient dedication to spiritual expectations. A resistance movement that began as a legitimate reaction to the thwarting of popular will, expressed along democratic lines, has degenerated into an orgy of competitive bestiality. State and quasi-state are locked in a deadly struggle, marked by a complete abandonment of the final vestiges of the norms of civilised society.

Such extremism could not stay localised for long. We have only to recollect that some of the leaders of this new insurgency cut their teeth in the struggle for the liberation of Afghanistan, a struggle that triumphed with the expulsion of Soviet forces of occupation from that nation, then recollect that such mujaheddin are pitted against a regime whose leaders are also veterans in the bruising war of liberation against French colonialism. And the consequence of these antecedents for global politics? The end of the notion of a nationalist war that would remain strictly within national confines. Perhaps such a notion had long since dissipated – only not much notice was paid at the time – dispelled by the Vietnam War, a war that sought no more than the liberation of its land from the domination of foreigners.

Regarding that war, I must express a puzzle. Vietnam,

then known as Indo-China, fought two wars of liberation, first from France, which she defeated at the famous battle of Dien-Bien Phu, then from the United States, which felt that she knew a thing or two that France did not. No one can forget the saturation bombing carried out by the United States in the latter stages of the war – a brutal assault that was actually described by the President, Richard Nixon, as an exercise to bomb North Vietnam to the negotiating table – nor the earlier barrage of defoliants whose effects have yet to wear off completely in that nation, the deadly chemical weapon, napalm, with horrendous images of inhuman disfiguration permanently seared on world memory. Now, the puzzle is this. I find it curious that the North Vietnamese, victims of two world powers in rapid succession, did not ever consider designating the entire world a war arena where innocents and guilty alike would be legitimately targeted. Not one incident of hijacking took place during those wars, neither did the taking of hostages, or the random detonation of bombs in places of tourist attraction or religious worship. United Nations agencies, as well as humanitarian organisations, appear to have enjoyed the respect due to neutrals in conflict. Most unbelievable of all, however, was the aftermath of that war, the now ritual encounters between US veterans and their former enemies in an embrace of reconciliation.

Certainly, during the entire Vietnam wars, it would have been an excessive claim to suggest that the world was trapped in a climate of fear. While we may dispute in the end what lessons must be drawn from this contrast, what remains certain is that it is one that needs to be closely studied. In the fifth lecture of this series – 'I am right; you are dead!' – we shall take this up again. Certainly we cannot ignore the antecedent histories of such peoples, their philosophies and their religions. The same observation may be made, albeit in a different vein, of the anti-apartheid struggle that was waged with no less commitment and intensity against a ruthless foe. The oppressed black people of South Africa did not pronounce the outside world guilty of the crime of continuing to survive while a majority race was being ground to earth by an implacable machinery of racist governance. There are hidden lessons in these studies in contrast, lessons that may enable us, after acknowledging the principal sources of the current climate of fear, to seek remedies that go beyond the rectification of the glaring and sustained conduct of global injustice.

It is always easy enough to address the material factors of conflict, and we do know that in most cases, such will be found as the primary causes. They can be identified and grasped, and usually provide a basis for negotiation even in the most intense moments of conflict. Nations fight over land, over water supply and other material resources and, in civil wars, also over political marginalisation – these are accessible causes of discontent, cogent in their manifestations. They go to the heart of a people's sense of social security and need for survival. Intermeshed with these, however, but not so intricately as to be totally inseparable, is a much neglected factor in its own right – the quotient of power, the will to dominate, to control, that strange impulse that persuades certain temperaments that they can realise their existence either individually or collectively only through the domination of others. We are speaking here of that phase when a struggle moves beyond its material causes – to restore parity within an exploitative order or whatever – and becomes one that is dedicated to the seizure and exercise of raw power. It goes to the heart of the phenomenon of those dictators who, long past their creative usefulness, still cling ruthlessly to the seat of power, a contemporary instance of which can be seen in the pitiable condition of the once revolutionary, now merely embarrassing ruler of Zimbabwe, whose rule is sustained today not by popular acceptance but by the agency of terror.

Let us not therefore limit the thrill of power only to its structured manifestations. The territorial – that is, the physical expression – of the will to dominate is only part of the story. There is also its furtive exercise, one that, often outgunned and outmanoeuvred, may even give up all interest in territorial control but will not give up the craving for domination. We may liken it to that now commonplace technological gadget known as the remote control, one that incidentally plays such a lethal role in the explosive dialogue of today's parties of conflict. We are speaking of the thrill of power by means other than actual governance, power as a pursuit in its own right, an addictive concentrate, extract or essence. It is a realm that need not be anchored in material grounds, remains a pursuit in its own right, craved for its own sake. The conduct of the child taunting and circumscribing the motions of a captive insect, or the well-known antics of the school bully – these are early forays into the laboratory of power, from where a taste may develop into major assaults on entire communities. The complementary emotion of the victim – insect or school pupil – that is, what the tormentor loves as reward is, of course, the expression of fear, accompanied by an abject surrender of volition.

I believe that it is time to confront a heightened reality – heightened, because not exactly new – and to include the factor of power, the instinct to power, among the motivating components of the human personality and social movements, an unquantifiable element that has always governed much of social and nation relationships. History concedes to exceptional figures, past and present – Alexander, Suleiman, King Darius, Chaka the Zulu, Ataturk, Indira Gandhi, etc. – the temperaments of nation-builders as well as nurturers of power. That latter impulsion is not glossed, neither by historians nor by the psychoanalysts of supermen and -women. What differs in our contemporary situation is that the relishing of power is no longer an attribute of the outstanding, exceptional individual, but is increasingly accessible even to the nondescript individual whose membership of a clique, or activities on behalf of the Chosen, more than fulfil this hunger for a share in the diet of power.

Is it strictly out of a commitment to the moral law —*Thou shalt not kill* — that the extreme anti-abortion crusader in the United States stalks and kills abortion doctors, patients and innocent passers-by, sometimes operating from within a network of protective cells? Or is there also an element of the thrill of membership of a quasi-state, exercising a form of power that transcends all mainstream social accords? We shall turn more fully to the theme of the Chosen in the fifth of these lectures.

For now, let me assure you that if you wish to observe the face of power at its most mundane, you do not have far to seek. You do not need to pay to see Marlon Brando in his role as the Godfather at the head of a Mafia combine. That face is omnipresent — from the clerical assistant on whom the emergence of a critical file depends, to anonymous members of an unacknowledged terrorist organisation in the United States known as the IRS — the Inland Revenue Service. Simply be on the receiving end of a letter of demand from that body to construct on your retina the driven personality of the writer!

Actually, that ogre has long since been displaced in my personal encounters — at least temporarily — by one of the new creatures of the heightened state of alert that now prevails in countries like the United States. These days, after you have checked in and gone through all the security checks, you may find yourself at the departure gate being subjected to a final, detailed check of your person and your baggage. That selection is mostly a random one, carried out by the computer. However, in other airports or, more accurately, with certain airlines, it is an airline security official who decides your fate either immediately before, or after, you have passed through the baggage-screening section. That individual, who presumably is trained not only in human but in document psychology, looks you up and down like some strange insect species, takes another look at your passport, weighs it in one hand or in both, and takes another look at you. She does not ask you any questions, all decisions are based on that dual inspection – of you and your documents. She pauses – there is a long queue behind you but she pauses a long while – to let you know that your fate is in her hands. Then, with the most contemptuous toss of her head, she indicates that you may go through, or ... step aside and join other lesser beings who are huddled, waiting to be stripped to their barest essentials. Don't take my word for it, go and see these individuals at work. There are a hundred ways I can think of – most of them actually polite and humane – whereby you can let a voyager know that you are about to subject him to some inconvenience, but for a laudable cause. No, these individuals let you know, in advance, that what you are about to experience is indignity, and that they, and they alone, are the powers that force-feed you this diet of humiliation.

I regret to have to inform you – and political correctness can go take a jump – that the nastiest, most obviously power-possessed officials that I have encountered in this manner have all been women, mostly between the ages of twenty and thirty, and – black! Perhaps the perennial war of the sexes is a factor, tied to the additional complication of the history of racism in the United States; I leave it to sociologists to look into this experience for me and offer their own explanations. All I do here is testify from experience – and on oath!

～

Let me not fail, simply for reasons of a deep, subjective, murderous loathing, to pay tribute to the creature to whom the modern crown of furtive power rightly belongs: the domination freak whose warped genius creates those invisible, proliferating Frankensteins from his dingy computer den and sends them in virtual space to invade and destroy the work of individuals and institutions. These aberrants are without an ounce of hatred in their veins, with no wrong to avenge, no cause to promote, with no physical or territorial ambition, indeed with no motivation other than the lust for power over unknown millions, both the meek and the powerful, the affluent and the deprived, the professor and the school pupil alike. I refer, of course, to none other than the cyber nerd, whose depredations we all must have felt at some time or other, or barely escaped. The most recent of these, like Mr 'Call Me God' the Maryland sniper, is not without a message for his captive world – 'Have the guts to call the name of Jesus' is the subject of the stalking horse on which his cannibal creation rides to wage his war of destruction on the unsuspecting.

It takes little imagination to picture this figure at his computer with, literally, the whole world at his finger-tips, locked in a competitive lust with unknown others for the power to inflict the maximum injury on humanity. Usually youthful, European or Asian – so report the cyber sleuths – and again PC be damned, this individual is of course impelled by a genuine passion for discovery, but the space between that motion of a tech-nological curiosity and the gesture that launches a virus on the world is the space that separates the explorer from the conqueror, the adventurer from the imperialist, the revolutionary from the dictator: it is the space of pure, unadulterated ecstasy of power.

Power, alas – even in its comic vein – is neither abstract nor metaphysical in its impact on society. The axis of tension between power and freedom continues to propel the very motions of personality development, social upheaval and nation conflicts. We must stress yet again that the urge to dominate may be the product of existing realities. Where such realities are not addressed, the political space is left fallow, enabling the calculating hand to fan the winds of fear. Some of these actualities may expand to threaten the peace of the world. Are they new, or are they simply the accentuation of well-known anomalies in nation relations? I began my remarks by deliberately identifying one such contributory breeding ground, Algeria. In forthcoming lectures, we shall touch on others – such as the Middle East – look into causes and effects, and perhaps even venture into speculations over possible solutions. I intend to proceed on the premise – one that I think is easy to agree upon – that humanity would rather work to dispel a climate of fear than live within it, and I assume also that we are equally agreed that, at this moment of speaking, we are well and truly enveloped in it. For now, let me devote the remaining time to taking us on a few turns along the axial relationship between power and freedom.

Science-fiction literature, of which I used to be an avid fan – I still am, it's just that I do not have as much time to indulge in it as I once had – as well as films in the same genre, is most instructive. Take *The Day of the Triffids*, where plants attempt to take over human society, or those films of alien body-snatchers, that most subversively imaginative way of taking over the key elements in a community, its government, progressively taking over the nation by assuming the physical shapes of a nation's ruling cadre. (Can we swear, by the way, that George Bush or Osama are not aliens in human shape?)

We may ask the question: in such fictions, what is the most basic element that twangs a chord of trepidation in the human viscera? Where does the reader, or viewer, identify most viscerally with the characters in this literary or cinematic genre? What gives that piquant edge to one's apprehension in much of science-fiction and horror literature? I suggest that it is very simply the notion of coming under the control of another being, of finding oneself dominated by an alien force, an alien bundle of values, sensibilities, tastes, agenda, beliefs and direction – in short, being robbed of one's social anchor. Apart from a fear of the loss of identity to those goblins from outer space – with heaven knows what nasty habits – one recognisable source of that repulsion is, very simply, the ancestral adversary of human freedom that we designate power. The goblin has taken over control of our existential volition.

Taking the foregoing together, we find that we need not wait to be visited or infiltrated by beings from outer space to arrive at the same state of fear and loathing that is associated with being manipulated by a force outside our own will. The vector of domination can, and constantly does, assail us in this here and present geographical environment. And we do know that in order to ensure absolute submission, that alien force must first lay a track of fear on which it rolls its juggernaut of domination. Even if the goals are not immediately articulated, may never be fully defined, power revels in first making itself manifest – then, other social themes may follow in its wake. May. Or may not. Power is self-sufficient, a replete possession, and must be maintained by whatever agency is required. We have already indicated that the readiest methodology to hand is the inculcation of fear. Ethiopia under Mariam Mengistu and the Dergue, Pinochet in Chile or Milosevic in former Yugoslavia, or the terror regime of the late General Sanni Abacha of Nigeria, all provide chilling contemporary testimonies of this relationship. Robert Mugabe of Zimbabwe is doing his best to ensure that the African continent remains relevant in the global study of this social phenomenon.

The mutual dependency of power and freedom has long been recognised, its consummation undertaken throughout the history of human association to the accompaniment of orgies of human sacrifice. Whether we believe in that reproductive miracle or not, it is useful to seize the nature of power as we do that of Immaculate Conception, an autogenous phenomenon – though one that can also be a product of willed imitation – and then we come to recognise more and more that, for its full savouring, power need not burden itself with such banal undertakings as social responsibility or restraints of morality. Every day, atrocities of once unimaginable dimensions remind us of this fact, events that are traceable to that moment when one individual, already in a rarefied existence of his own, salivates over an exquisite moment of fulfilment as he watches his victims, mostly already existing in that half-life of social invalidation – the other half being mortgaged to the fear of the unexpected – squirm in awe of his efficacy of control. Surely it is not a merely fabulous projection that sees such an individual, alone in his or her hermetic world, suffused with an inward smile of satisfaction: *'Now, you lot, I have you in my power. At this moment, I, and I alone, know, and am about to decide your fate.'*

$\sim$

I no longer recall the title of the film that was made of the Red Brigade in Italy, after the abduction and murder of a Prime Minister, Aldo Moro, who was out of power at the time. If we may leave aside the dubious politics of that assassination, and the movement of which these formed a part, what remains ineluctable is the study in smug self-righteousness of his abductors, as they proceeded to decide the fate of their prisoner. Blame the director, if you wish, for failing to extract a sense of ideological *necessity, inevitability,* in the decision that was taken to eliminate him. What came through instead – perhaps it was the director's intention anyway – was the sense of a 'hallowed space' as the dominant environment of the revolutionary cell, an evocation of the unreal that was accentuated by the real psychological extract, the autonomy of power, conveyed in the demeanour of these mostly young individuals. This all-pervasive extract was, in my view, the exercise of power. These individuals, separated from a world that they genuinely despised, or affected to despise, were lodged in the hermetic enclosure of absolutism. A limited environment, yes, but an environment that they totally controlled, and of which they were the privileged janitors. This was what mattered most. They were not deciding the fate of an individual, not even of a symbol, I felt, but were simply engrossed in the exercise of secretive dominance, and this was what lent that film its bleak and pathetic intensity. One was transported into another world whose basic commodity, evenly shared within the circle of the Chosen, and celebrated with all due ritual and solemnity, was simply – power. Unnamed, unacknowledged, power was none the less the palpable fetish of worship.

Well, theorising apart, the young executioners, imbued with a sense of a 'holy mission', or simply wallowing – albeit with all appearance of deep reflection – in the pure ambience of power, left the Western, capitalist world in no doubt whatsoever about their essential product: a climate of fear that enveloped the moneyed, their relations, the remotely connected, the political class, the middle class and, occasionally, innocent victims of what military language loves to gloss as 'collateral damage'.

I must continue to insist that we do not underestimate the relevance of a material base – even justification – of the 'holy mission' in all of this. However, even the most evidently objectivised base of the 'holy mission' is often complicated by the sheer relish that is experienced in the control of others. It is not possible to reject absolutely the notion that one – just one in four, in ten, in two dozen – may be governed by no more than an impulse to secret, furtive dominance, the fulfilment of that individual by a moment of self-abandonment to this mysterious essence of power. I know, because I have met some such individuals. So, I am certain, have others in this audience. For now, I could do worse than attempt to burrow into the core of this commodity, one that has remained a puzzle to psychologists and philosophers – Hegel, Hobbes, Nietzsche and all – and, as with all riddles of the human condition and social impulses, leaves one with more questions than answers. It becomes an almost obsessive quest for some clarifying clues, illuminating – not more obscurantist speculations – when one has been a participant in the kind of deadly struggle that ensues when one individual, a single mortal with no discernible exceptional qualities, convinces himself that it is his mission to bludgeon a populace of some millions

– ten, twenty, forty, a hundred or more millions – into submission.

So now, directly to that conundrum – power – just what is that? We know what it does. For a start, power takes away the freedom of the other and replaces it with fear. Still, that does not answer the ontological question. What, we may ask, is the common factor, the ingredient that guarantees a trill of nervous apprehension in, on the one hand, an audience watching *Dr Strangelove* and, on the other, the citizens of Maryland with a sniper on the loose? Power, of course. The primitive fear of being controlled. It does not matter whether it is an invasion from outer space or power wielded from a subterranean command post: some alien force is about to take control of us, to dominate – and, if necessary in the process, to terminate our existence. We never stop to think – or, at best, a secondary consideration is whether such a force might be for the good, that humanity might indeed be improved by such a takeover. Volition, to which we desperately cling, is the very definition of our mature completion as social beings. The basis of rejection that registers itself in an audience seated at a theatrical or cinematic representation of the megalomaniac has always been the antithesis of human volition – power!

We have known it also described as a sexual substitute or an aphrodisiac, but this only begs the question. Victims of rape often take a different position. Next to the horror of bodily violation, a frequent admission by victims is of the humiliation of being totally subjected to another's control. And the more sadistic the rapist, the greater his urge to exact an acknowledgement from the victim of submission to his dominance. Sexual gratification is of course at the heart of such violations, but pre-eminent is the satisfaction of dominating another, making him or her totally subject to his whims, some of which may not even be sexual in nature. In whatever proportion we choose to present these cravings, there is no question that a sense of power generates its own satisfaction, and is an important element in the drive towards rape. So, once again, back to the question – just what *is* power?

Is it perhaps no more than a deadly mutation of ambition, one that may or may not translate into social activity? Any fool, any moron, any psychopath can aspire to the seizure and exercise of power, and of course the more psychopathic, the more efficient: Hitler, Pol Pot, Idi Amin, Sergeant Doe and the latest in the line of the unconscionably driven, our own lately departed General Sanni Abacha – all have proved that power, as long as you are sufficiently ruthless, amoral and manipulative, is within the grasp of even the mentally deficient. So, power is really neither efficacy nor a mandatory facilitator of vision or political purpose. Of course the pursuit of power may be impelled by vision, but power in itself is not to be mistaken for vision. On the contrary, true vision may eschew power, may totally repudiate power, seeking to fulfil itself by that hardy, self-sacrificial route that does not lean on the crutch of power. There are individuals in every field of human endeavour who have pursued their vision, and in a multiplicity of fields – to the benefit of millions and tens of millions around the world – without that promiscuous facilitator named power. And power, let us stress just once more, need not be an individual aspiration; it can be no more than mere participation in a collective exercise, a variant that is the intriguing and proliferating arm of hegemonic obsession of a unit within a totality.

Since I do not believe that we shall ever arrive at a satisfactory explication of power, I have settled for that functional one – that is, a definition that enables us to proceed to the social neutralisation of this affliction whenever it rears its head. After all, the manifestation of raw power is an encounter that is inevitable right from infancy, and through the normal course of existence – be it in a rainstorm, the force of lightning, or an earthquake. Even the casual wind that takes down a rotten branch or a roof or two is a manifestation of the hidden force of Nature that suddenly exercises its authority from time to time, and without any intervention from man. Nature, therefore, sometimes reveals herself as a pure expression of power – and it is perhaps somewhat more than an anthropomorphic conceit to suggest that man, in those activities that incline him towards the exercise of dominance, is merely attempting a crude appropriation in response to that elemental attribute that is an expression of the very forces that surround and threaten to overwhelm him, not least of which is mortality.

In short, power is, paradoxically, the primordial marshland of fear, from which emerges the precipitate of man's neurotic response to mortality. Therein he proceeds to attempt to match himself with the force of Nature, that agency through which the various apprehensions of God, Super Being, or whatever name — including Death — are filtered. You cannot, however, contain within yourself the elemental force of death, godhead, a thunderstorm, an earthquake or a volcano, never mind the comparison of some energetic types to a whirlwind. Those who take such metaphors personally are subject matter for traditional psychiatry, and it is for this reason that ancient societies devised a number of ritualised scenarios for the banalisation of power. As a dramatist, I have myself experimented with a number of rituals towards that end. Here is one — designed, however, only for the formal, not the shadowy counterpart of manifest power. It takes off from the French playwright and exorcist Jean Genet.

A glitzy brothel, most appropriately, is the setting for Jean Genet's ritualisation of the promiscuous facilitator — power — in his play *The Balcony*. There, the power-obsessed come periodically to act out their fantasies. Here now is a summary of my variation on Jean Genet:

Suppose we modernised Genet's rather primitive stage mechanics to embrace the very latest in special effects, *à la* Steven Spielberg. Society would proceed to offer its ruler a chance to erupt with the earthquake, soar on flues of the thunderstorm and become virtually one with the convulsion that attends the birth of new planets. Encased in a Virtual Reality capsule, a super Jacuzzi, the Maximum Leader would dominate the universe every day before breakfast. As a finale – and here I must acknowledge the inspiration of the innovation of that late leader Mobutu Sese Seko of Zaire, who soared with the sunrise and disappeared into the clouds every morning on his nation's television – the Leader would watch the daily waste of his bodily functions morph into a celestial orb – the sun, no less – rising over the horizon, approving the beginning of a new day for his people.

After such an immersion in the utter sublimity of galactic power, any mortal must emerge with nothing but contempt for the mere pittance of awe and terror that are the normal dues from his miserable subjects. He would leave them – us – to wallow in our now unappealing state of … unbroken freedom, and the absence of fear.

I am persuaded that this is a ritualistic offering that no man-eating dictator, with the innate theatrics of that breed, could ever refuse.

3

Rhetoric that binds
and blinds

I propose to address this topic from two directions –
one, the political; the other, the religious. Given the fact
that, in the present day – and indeed, in a nearly
unbroken continuum of history – both often prove to
be merely two sides of the same coin, it should not be
surprising if, from time to time, it would indeed appear
that all we are engaged upon is tossing up, just like a
coin, one two-sided notion. We watch it spin through
the air in a blur of rapid alternations, and succumb the
law of gravity – known as coming down to earth – to
reveal one side or the other, near interchangeably. The
sanctimoniousness that often characterises one – the
political – on the one hand, and the sacrosanctity that

is claimed as the foundation of the other, even when it extends its constituency to the political and the mundane, make it clear that they are both claimants to the same highway of influence and control of human lives whose ultimate destination is power – the consolidation of power in itself, or the execution of policies that aspire to the total control of a polity.

Thus, the president of a powerful nation addresses a political situation in what amounts to revelationary language tinged with messianism. Nearly on the other side of the globe, a religious leader whips up his citizens in a frenzy of alarm whose tenor is that the very salvation of their collective soul – and only incidentally the survival of the state – is jeopardised. In the hysterical condition that is aroused in the populace, hundreds of youths are sentenced to be hanged for the crime of being 'agents of Satan', 'enemies of God' and so on. Back again to the other side, wars of dubious justification are launched, humanity is savaged, the globe destabilised, and all rhetoricians of power sleep soundly, until it is time for the next hysterical whip-up. The coupling within 'for God and country' is no historic accident.

Let me, as we proceed, call attention to the fact that hysteria is not always an outwardly-expressed abnormality, usually loud and violent. In fact, there is the quiet form of hysteria, as medical experts will testify. Hysteria can also manifest itself as a collective and infectious outbreak, one that cannot always be accurately traced to a logical causative event. At its most affective, it emerges as the product of a one-way communication – a monologue, in short – that succeeds in blinding its followers to the very realities that surround them while sealing them in a community of conviction, even of the unresolved kind. That condition is indifferent to verification of the content of what is being communicated, indifferent to the moralities or justice – if any – of its claims, or the probable consequences of its pursuit. The moment is all, and creates for each affected member a highly solipsistic existence within a charmed circle, whose only reference point is that infinite moment of mass excitation. The rhetorical hysteria that is produced in such circumstances often dissipates soon after, but not always. Numbers promise more than safety as in 'safety in numbers' – they often guarantee certitude and invulnerability. Thus the collective conviction that sustains the individual may be dissipated with the physical dispersal of the crutch of numbers – let us say, after a political or religious rally. In such a case, the pathology of the moment is redressed by a return to reality, and each individual regains his or her whole being – until the next time.

However, a hard core of the message embedded in that emotive ferment may linger on, resulting in individual recalls, at various levels of consciousness, of the basic tenor of the collective experience, urging on the execution of its embedded message. The core of retention may be beatific, resulting in a resolve to improve the lot of a long-neglected neighbour, make restitution where some illegality has been committed, or an immoral advantage secured. It can lead to a grandiose vision for the betterment or salvation of mankind. The religious variety is prone to generating such aftermath, a Moral Rearmament longing of one kind or another. On the other hand, alas, it may produce the very opposite, the destructive and apocalyptic. The ideological route is an equally mixed bag, but usually more disruptive, more contradictory, since it lays claim to rational processes, yet acts with the dogmatism of the purely revelational.

What I have referred to as rhetorical hysteria may therefore be safely considered the product of a one-way communication; that is, the monologue or public harangue. Dialogue, on the other hand, actually involves exchange, and the circumstances must be very abnormal indeed when it results in the hysterical condition. It is both convenient and relevant to personify, at this point, the difference between these two through the contrasting personalities of the late Ayatollah Khomeini, and others of like temper, and the current, embattled leader of Iran, President Khomeini. We shall return to this most instructive pair towards the end.

It would also help, perhaps, if we advanced our exploration of the rhetorical theme through the terrain of light relief, if only to nudge the more self-assured nations, movements and religions in the direction of a sense of proportion, by reflecting their certitudes through escapades that are often no more than self-indulgent gambits, an infectious assertiveness that they would prefer to despise as simplistic mimicries of their own more elaborate, better-structured, packaged and advanced manifestos. What often develops to the level of rhetorical hysteria may begin as small pinpricks designed to annoy a complacent society and perhaps reinforce a group feeling of dissidence, but may develop into veritable monstrosities of absolute notions that run amok, consuming all within sight until they eventually consume themselves or are consumed by more rabid challengers. I shall share my favourite example, but not just yet. First, we should establish the socio-political background and context, just to situate ourselves in the general ambience of its times.

Many here will still recall that leftist phase of the sixties, labelled Trotskyite or Maoist, one that is now being superseded by other radical motions towards the transformation of man and society. It is a phase that is now receding into obscurity, thanks mostly to the collapse of communist ideology. I happen to believe that the humanistic foundation of the socialist ideal has not been thereby invalidated, but this belongs to another discourse entirely. In any case, the passion for a basis in ideological righteousness is still daily manifested in isolated anarchic acts against society, as well as in ideo-logically-based wars around the globe. The period that I wish to recall was characterised by the exploits of the Red Brigade based largely in Italy, Action Directe in France, the Baader-Meinhof in Germany etc., with clones in Latin America and Japan, in addition to one or two isolated spots in Asia. Perhaps the most sensational single event of that period was the kidnapping and murder of the former Italian Prime Minister Aldo Moro. Kidnapping of businessmen or their relations for ransom was commonplace, nor can one easily forget the ruthless, cult-style executions in hidden mountain caves of Japan for alleged crimes of deviation from the pure strain of the revolutionary ideal. Not too surprisingly, other variants resulted in convoluted alliances between ideological and criminal impulses – drug-trafficking allied to radical idealism in countries like Colombia.

The famous youth-inspired 1968 uprising in Paris that attempted to resurrect a commune modelled after the Paris Commune of the French revolutionary ferment was another notable manifestation of the passion for change, a severe testing of the status quo, and very French in temper, despite its continental alliances. Other names like Red Danny, Cohn-Bendit, Regis Debray, Angela Davis etc. entered the lore of world revolutionary gladiators, satellites in orbit around the ultimate symbol of the times – Che Guevara. Depending on which arc of the class spectrum one occupied, and the methodology of action advocated and deployed, the overall movement evoked among the world population extreme degrees of admiration, revulsion – and fear. How wide would the movement spread, especially among youth? How deeply would it undermine the fabric of society?

This, then, was the setting for a far less sensational but widely diffuse offshoot of the same cast of mind – the junior partners, if you like – that had sprung up within the radical atmosphere of the sixties. It is the extract, a proliferating mantra from the diffuse, non-lethal offshoots, that I wish to identify as typifying the nature of rhetoric that, in varying degrees of flippancy and adolescent conviction, can graduate over time into an agenda for unreflective extremism, building up to a hysterical level that turns an otherwise rational section of humanity into active conduits for, at the very least, a mandatory suspension of disbelief. It is a phenomenon that reveals itself in its abandonment of scepticism. A new community is born, imbued with its own moral code – again, not one that is subjected to rigorous tests – that places itself outside existing social arrangements. A complacent society views them at first with a condescending amusement, later with trepidation.

How I came to observe this process at first hand was just as relevant to my observations. I was in self-imposed exile, a therapy I had embarked upon for another situation of lethal rhetorics that had sacrificed a million or two of Nigerian humanity under the rhythmic mantra: *To keep the nation one is a task that must be done.* Our civil war was being concluded in a mood of euphoria and, as I emerged from prison detention, I was not sure which form of hysteria grated more – the tone of nationalist jingoism that had surrounded me before I was locked up, one that made that war inevitable in the first place, or the barely suppressed triumphalist smugness into which I was thrust as I regained my freedom. Military success was equated with a divine vindication of the war.

On the other side, in the breakaway Biafran state, the same syndrome had more tragic results. Youths went into battle with nothing but wooden guns in their hands, captives of the same rhetoric that was drummed daily into their heads – *No power on the African continent can subdue us.* That belief had somehow translated into the mimic guns with which they charged the federal foe, as reported by a colleague who pronounced himself numbed by the experience. Was it any different, I wondered, from the self-submission of normally hard-headed men to the rhetorical powers of a Ugandan, Alice Lakwena, and her Army of the Lord? Alice's volunteers charged into hails of bullets, convinced that they were immune to their penetration, that the force of bullets was neutralised as a result of the inoculation that Alice administered to them. After the capture of Alice in Tanzania, a university professor who had been part of her army was asked, in an interview, how it was possible for him, a man of presumed intellect, to have been persuaded of the supernatural powers of this woman, and for so long. He could proffer no answer, only that he supposed that they had all been under some spell. Fatalities, he said, had been rationalised away – such victims were only the weak in faith. This scenario has been sadly encountered in many more civil-war zones all over the continent, most especially among the child soldiers.

～

And now we come to the nurturing environment of the mantra. As I began my lecture tour of some European universities during that exile, it did not take long for me to realise that the mood of the historic Paris uprising was still in the ascendant, never mind the failure of that movement – and perhaps the zeal, being all that was left, was even more wilfully embraced on that account. I came into daily contact with students and all manner of disenchanted youths seeking a revolutionary answer to the inequalities, the oppressive contradictions of their societies. Maoists, or Maoist-Leninists, or Troskyites, Proudhonists, or Maoist-Leninists-Troskyites, Stalinist-Leninists … no matter what hyphenated revolutionary tendencies they professed, all had one fundamental trait in common. They were bearers of a new illumination on the condition and future of human society. They were the subversive agents who would topple the bourgeois order and liberate 'the new man' with all his potential, unfettered by the norms of a failed society, its hypocrisies and dubious ethical values. They formed a compact of solidarity with the marginalised no matter how remotely placed – from the bauxite mines of Jamaica to the coal mines of South Africa. Ideologically schooled in Marxism, even at its most rudimentary, most did not directly espouse anarchism as a social philosophy, but gave a practical, anarchic demonstration of the cue they had elicited from Karl Marx's analysis of law: law was not neutral, but was an instrument to protect the interests of the ruling classes. In a class struggle, therefore, which it was their avowed mission, indeed their duty, to initiate, law itself was to be repudiated.

As for wealth, from where did wealth emanate but from the exploitation of man by man, proven by the immoral profit from the surplus labour of others? Thus, logically, their enabling mantra, based on the authority of Karl Marx, which declared quite simplistically that *All property is theft*. That slogan was put into practice in any number of ways, from the merely self-dramatising gesture to the socially disruptive, once it was placed in tandem with Marx's interpretation of law, which could now be taken as advocating its own overthrow.

In Germany or France of the late sixties to early seventies, a student who took a parked bicycle, motor bike or motor car that belonged to another did not consider it an act of theft. He kept it and returned it at his leisure, or simply kept it for as long as it took him to acquire a more attractive or convenient one, abandoning the former hundreds of kilometres from where its owner last saw it. Libraries bewailed their helplessness as students took away books and never returned them, often returning to exercise their right to 'borrow' some more. Others felt that the shelves of bookstores should be open to the acquisitive mood of the reader. Students felt quite noble in raiding the accounts of a parent or guardian – or indeed the neighbourhood store. *All property is theft* – and that, do take note, included intellectual property. In short, plagiarism was no crime.

I recall an incident in my own university in Ibadan, Nigeria, where a radicalised section of the student body had also caught the fever. If my former students are listening, I hope they will excuse me – I promise that this is the last time I shall make use of this incident, but it was a most revealing episode for me at the time, given my own search for an ideological anchor within the troubled and questing post-colonial generation in my own society. In any case, it is simply too juicy a recollection for me to abandon so easily! There was a protest demonstration; I no longer recall the cause, but it grew violent. In the process, a professor whose role was considered objectionable during the crisis became a target of the students' ire and a prime candidate for 'revolutionary justice' – another of those rhetorical devices embraced by states in their post-revolution phase and adopted by radical movements. The professor's house on campus was invaded and vandalised, then his office. His research papers were set on fire. Later, I tackled some of the students: why, I demanded, had they gone so far as to destroy what was, in effect, the life-work of this senior colleague (whose politics, incidentally, I also despised)? The reply I received was straight from the European revolutionary cookbook that I had encountered in Paris or Frankfurt: intellectual property, they declared, is not the product of any one individual; thus, the professor had no personal claims to anything that was lost.

That same tendency – albeit by no means of the same pyromaniacal temper – was echoed at the time by radical caucuses in Europe and the United States. It gave rise to the buzzword 'collective'. Even performance groups were no longer acting companies or drama troupes, but 'collectives'. A famous American author caught the fever. She went – for a while – to the extreme extent of refusing to credit her own person with authorship of her books: it was the work of collective humanity, she declared, and she was merely the humble medium through whom these insights were expressed. It was one of those revivalist periods of the thoughtful, committed but guilt-laden left – personal proprietorship of any kind had become the original sin. I recall meeting her during this period and asking her how she resolved the issue of collectivism when it came to the distribution of royalties. Frankly, I do not remember that she provided any satisfactory answer.

This was an infectious, but only mildly misleading

eruption of the rhetorical hysteria that overtook radicalised minds all over the world, one that was characterised by a one-dimensional approach to all faces of reality, however varied or internally contradicting. The most dangerous of these catch-phrases has surely resurfaced in the minds of many of us in contemporary times: *There are no innocents!* Yes, it was prevalent even then. The sixties and seventies mood of extreme militancy, its repudiation of all 'bourgeois morality', a natural proceeding from the logic of the class-subservient interests of law, led remorselessly to the tacit, sometimes loudly-argued endorsement of acts of sabotage, kidnapping and even murder. At the time, the self-willed hysteria was induced by a deliberate exercise of blinding the mind to other considerations, screaming doubts into silence. Sometimes it was a silent scream, inaudible, but it was one that was none the less *legible* on the faces of a number in any crowd of those 'conscientisation' sessions if one was not caught up within the rhetorical fervour. The sessions were closer in temper to a Billy Graham religious revivalism than to the models that they sought to emulate, such as Fidel Castro's famous marathons.

Shall we take one more? It would be a great pity to leave out a revolutionary favourite of that infectious season of liberation, whose total, self-sacrificial idealism was certainly shared by many of us in that generation, indeed, must be regarded as inevitable, given the circumstances of colonial repressions: *Power grows from the barrel of a gun* – attributed to Mao Zedong. It filled the revolutionary airwaves, but, even if this were a truthful absolute – and I use this only as an illustration of the elisions that are inbuilt into the rhetorical structure – what was conveniently suppressed were the innumerable contradictions and cautions of the dialectical propositions that would arise effortlessly from such a thesis, and which strike us today, in hindsight, with such demonstrable force from one continent to another. I refer to potentially inhibitory discoveries of history and society, such as *Power corrupts, and absolute power corrupts absolutely.* Nowhere was this more robustly exemplified than in the Soviet Union and its empire, which were held up as fulfilment of radical absolutes that sometimes proved little more than rhetorical devices. There is room for dialectical thought within rhetoric – indeed, rhetoric may be reinforced by legitimate syllogisms – but the heady rhetoric whose goal is mass hysteria is not designed to pause for sequences of logical, even if purely theoretical, deductions.

Is it any surprise that the new purveyors of fear of our time have moved beyond submission to such rational scrutiny? They are not the student cafeteria crowd, or the Sunday-afternoon rhetoricians of Speakers' Corner in London's Hyde Park, who, after all, return home and re-digest, and debate what has been proposed. They are creatures not of uncertainty but of holy conviction, and they have demonstrated again and again that they consider their lives of value only when they expend them – not even incidentally, but in a deliberate act guaranteed to take the maximum toll on innocents – as the ultimate consummation of that conviction. Not for them the Buddhist route of a limited self-immolation as the ultimate statement, as was prevalent in South Korea under the reign of dictatorial incontinence. These belong to a most select, near impenetrable community, from within whose ranks power, even posthumously, grows from the suicide bomb.

There are no innocents: this accentuation of the earlier rhetoric – *All property is theft* – which makes us all thieves since we claim life as property, however temporarily, is what marks the difference between the rhetorical hysteria that held the world in thrall in those fervid sixties and seventies, on the one hand, and the nature of what we are witnessing today. Combine those two limited shorthand rhetorical triggers and we move to the zone of the catechism that claims that *All life is theft*, and thus should be restored to its legitimate owner by any true believer, and as rapidly as possible. If only we could persuade the apostles of such gospels of the infinite justice of leaving such restoration to the personal intervention of the divine proprietor! Alas, they have constituted themselves agents of restitution, where innocents pay sudden forfeit, without even the consolation of seeking assurance of divine forgiveness for the lamentable lapse of living.

~

The question we must now confront is this: who or what are the principal agents of the season of rhetorical hysteria that now seek to bind and blind the world within our climate of fear?

We need a lot of objectivity, and a commitment to equitable dealing, in addressing this question. Fortunately – but what a costly piece of fortune! – the world has received a most exemplary piece of instruction in the devastating potential of the private addiction to a rhetorical condition that can spread and infect a whole nation. For this, we must thank the President of one of the most powerful nations of the world, the United States. For an intense period that began a year or more ago, our airwaves were bombarded with an entrapment piece of monologue of just four words – *weapons of mass destruction*. It was a sustained demonstration, both as metaphor and as prophecy, of how empty such rhetoric can prove, yet how effectively it can blind a people, lead them into a cul-de-sac, securing nearly an entire nation within a common purpose that proves wrongly premised. Outside that nation itself, more than a few others were swept up in the hysteria that was stimulated by no more than the simple but passionate evocation of that mantra, *weapons of mass destruction*. Predictably, it was only a matter of time before it acquired an acronym – WMD – either for ease of reference, or perhaps as a relief for that unco-operative mantra that stubbornly refused to manifest its name. WMD aspired to the level of religious faith. Individuals who disputed its claimed reality found themselves subjected to abuse, sometimes of a violent nature. Both overtly and indirectly, unbeliever nations were either offered inducements or threatened with sanctions.

The hysteria that was inspired by that presidential monologue echoed, for many, the McCarthy period of anti-communist hysteria, when the mere failure to denounce the communist ideology with satisfactory fervour, or to denounce one's colleagues for communist sympathies, became an unpatriotic act that was sometimes accounted treason. Thus came into being the damning tag *unAmerican activities*, to ferret out and punish which a standing committee was set up in the United States legislature. Was there any difference between that rhetorical device of the mid-fifties and that of the turn of this century? Certainly there has been continuity. To ensure that the nation co-option that fed on the rhetoric of 'the enemy within' did not lack for nourishment, the decades between *unAmerican activities* and *weapons of mass destruction* were caulked with holding devices of the nature of 'Evil Empire' and, latterly, 'Axis of Evil'. The beauty of the political mantra has always been its ability to distil complex events and global relationships into a rhetorical broth that precludes digestion, but guarantees satisfaction.

~

Let no one underestimate the criminal immensity of September 11, 2001, that arrogant manifestation of the mantra *There are no innocents,* nor its hideous impact on global consciousness. The tasteless gloating of a handful of normally astute writers and intellectuals whose will to radicalism sometimes overpowers their humanism is only a measure of the pretentious detachment of some of us from the world we live in, and should not be permitted to cloud our individual revulsion over that event, any more than it should inhibit us from interrogating the choices of response that could be expected from the leadership of a stricken people. More than sufficient time has elapsed for objective consideration of the choices, with all due allowance also made for the fact that it was *that* space, not ours, that was most directly affected, most deeply traumatised, most deeply and forcibly injected with the virus of fear.

There were options, however, and the case is being made here that the leadership of that nation chose to substitute, for a hard assessment of its relationship with the rest of humanity, an emotive rhetoric that blinded it even further, driving that nation deeper into an isolationist monologue, even within the debating chambers of the United Nations. Afghanistan of the Taliban, sheltering and collaborating with the murderous quasi-state of Al Queda, had declared direct war on a people and thus richly deserved its comeuppance. However, the rhetorical momentum engendered since the monstrous date of September 11 has propelled the United States into an unjustifiable war in Iraq. A global wave of sympathy has been frittered away in a defiant unilateralism that appears to thrive on hysteria and deception. We have watched and listened in recent times to the unedifying acts and pronouncements of a nation that is not accustomed to being contradicted, deeming it a heresy on the part of any nation or world figure to balk at intoning the mantra of *weapons of mass destruction*.

Reprisals from the nation that draped its shoulders in a mantle of infallibility attained some bemusing dimensions. The greatest umbrage against the restraining community of sceptics was reserved for France, whose cultural penetration of the United States was more prolific in symbols of snobbishness than that of her partner in crime, the Republic of Germany. Germany got off quite lightly. To the intense embarrassment of a substantial minority of Americans themselves, a number of restaurants that once proudly advertised themselves as French quickly changed their names or painted out the French tricolour designs outside their establishments. Nowhere is it recorded that any thought was given to the nation's Canadian neighbour, which recognises herself as bicultural. America's law-making chambers took 'French fries' off their cafeteria menu and renamed that item 'Freedom chips'. The French baguette and croissants lost out to sourdough bread, bagels and pretzels. Most incredible of all, many wine shops and bars threw out their stock of French wines, depleted their shelves as rapidly as they could by selling them at rock-bottom prices, where they were gleefully gobbled up by infidels to the gospel of WMD – among whom was most certainly a cash-strapped Nobelist who shall remain nameless. It was either you believed in weapons of mass destruction or you became overnight a pariah. It did not matter in the least that these WMD faithfuls understood that this was a dangerous religion that would not end in mere rhetoric but that guaranteed, from the very beginning, a denouement not simply of war, but of war-lust. The triumph of the monologue was supreme.

There are moments, it must be admitted, when the imperatives of dialogue appear to be foreclosed. Nevertheless, we dare not stop contrasting the dangers of the monologue with the creative potentials of its alternative, the latter holding out a chance of contracting, if not completely dissipating, our climate of fear. Certainly, the proliferation of this frame of mind can slow down the division of the world into two irreconcilable camps, and hopefully prevent such a division from taking permanent hold. Fortunately, a global awareness of the perilous consequences of avoidance is not missing and, thus, provides us with a positive note on which to end, invoking the lessons in contrast between two figures who may be held to personify the two polarities – monologue and dialogue. Both of them, most usefully, are products of the same history, the same religion, the same culture and the same nation state. I therefore invite you to accompany me to a milestone event that took place in the United Nations, with its symbolic timing for the end of the last millennium, an event that declared, in ringing terms, that it was time to eschew the sterile monologues of the past and cultivate a new spirit of dialogue, the only prescription that the world knows for the hysterical affliction that belongs to its adversary, the monologue.

The event was the elaborate inauguration of the project Dialogue of Civilisations at the United Nations headquarters in New York, attended by several heads of state, other world leaders, intellectuals, ministers of religion and so on. There it was that President Khatami of Iran, the main sponsor of the project – in partnership with UNESCO – delivered a most enlightened speech, one that, I am certain, took his audience by surprise. On the minds of most of that audience, including mine, was unquestionably the keen awareness that we were listening to the leader of that same nation which, not quite a decade earlier, had imposed on the world a new era of fear by a unilateral appropriation of the power of life and death over any citizen of our world, as he

77

pronounced a death *fatwa* on the writer Salman Rushdie for his alleged offence against his religion, Islam. A major religion, deservedly classified as one of the world religions, but, just the same, only one of the structures of transcendental intimations, or superstitions, known as religion.

It is not my intention here to pursue the rights and wrongs of the province of the imagination, certainly not my intention to berate or defend a writer accused of disrespect or insensitivity towards religious belief. My concern today is simply to call attention to the contrasting activities of the leadership of that country, Iran, in a truly elevating mission to restore dialogue to its rightful place as an agent of civilisations. Also, it is necessary to remind ourselves that the consequences of that precedent of a global incitement to murder are still very much with us, a poisoned watershed in the relationships between and within nations. It has contributed to a large extent to the very condition of global intolerance, bigotry and sectarian violence to whose dismantling an elected Iranian leader now committed himself in the halls of the United Nations. All over the world, with a frequency, frenzy and impunity that did not exist before the Salman Rushdie affair, a Friday sermon in a mosque over a real or imagined slight has led to mayhem in normally harmonious communities, in places stretching from Kaduna and the Plateau State in Nigeria to hitherto obscured Indonesian regions such as Aceh.

Some may consider this timing a coincidence; if so, it is a coincidence that some of us did anticipate and openly predict at international gatherings.

A dismal instance within my own nation, Nigeria, was that of the governor of a largely Muslim state in the north, Zamfara, who catapulted himself into international notoriety by this mimic route, pronounced a killing *fatwa* on a young journalist. Her crime? A comment that the Prophet Muhammad did not lack an eye for beauty in womanhood. This alleged insult, in addition to claims of provocation in the staging of a Miss World beauty pageant whose so-called female immodesty a handful of zealots insisted was an affront to their religious sensibilities, led to the destabilisation of the country's capital city, Abuja, and the unleashing of an orgy of death and destruction that stunned the world in its mindlessness and ferocity. Like a number of others around the globe, mine was a nation that, once upon a time, indeed as recently as forty years ago, could offer herself as a model of tolerance, but has suffered, in the intervening period, a spate of religion-motivated violence on an unprecedented scale, and is fast becoming only another volatile zone of distrust, unease and tension.

We have a duty therefore to use every opportunity to disseminate efforts that counteract such moments of divisiveness and retrogression. President Khatami's challenge has been taken up in several fora, even to the extent of the emergence of a permanent NGO – Dialogue of Civilisations. Still lacking, however, is a manifest global commitment, especially a sustained and dynamic reciprocity from rival cultures and religions. The word of course is 'dynamic' – perhaps I should even use the word 'aggressive'. The globe needs to be saturated, almost on a daily basis, with such encounters. There have been a number, admittedly, including one in Georgia of the former Soviet Union, under the same rubric as Dialogue; another in Macedonia. Others have taken place within Iran as well. I participated in one in Abuja, Nigeria, in December last year, the scene of the religion-instigated massacre to which I earlier referred.

Sadly, it is within the religious domain that the phenomenon of rhetorical hysteria takes its most devastating form. I am aware that, in some minds, this tends to be regarded as a delicate subject. Let me declare very simply that I do not share such a sentiment. There is nothing in the least delicate about the slaughter of innocents. We all subscribe to the lofty notions contained in the Universal Declaration of Human Rights but, for some reason, become suddenly coy and selective when it comes to defending what is obviously the most elementary of these rights, which is *the right to life*. One of my all-time favourite lines comes from the black American poet Langston Hughes. It reads, simply, 'There is no lavender word for lynch'. Now, that is one line I would not mind converting to the service of rhetorical hysteria. It leaves no room for the continuation of the culture of impunity currently enjoyed by – literally – sacred cows.

Our experiences in Nigeria – shared by numerous others – testify to the frequency of the lamentable conversion of the mantra of piety to the promotion of the most hideous form of impiety, which, in my catechism, translates as the slaughter of other human beings in the cause of religious or any other conviction. For those of us who grew up in an atmosphere where the first dawn sounds that lulled one out of sleep were the sounds of the muezzin – the jarring loudspeakers had not yet been co-opted – calling his flock to the first prayer of the day, soon to be intermingled with the chant of the Christian creed from the catechist's household next door, it is an agonising reversal to watch the faces of fanatics slavering after blood under the mandates of those same incantations. Those of us who are unlikely ever to be found intoning, either alone or amidst a congregation, those familiar spiritual calls such as *Praise Jesus, Hallelujah, Allah akbar, Hare Krishna* and so on should at least be permitted to retain whatever memories we have of these religions in their non-aggressive states, share the inspirational value that others clearly derive from them, and indeed continue to nurse even a frag-mented faith in their potential for human regeneration. But we also have a duty to challenge a general reluctance to enquire why the adherents of some religions more than others turn the pages of their scriptures into a divine breath that fans the random homicidal spore to all corners of the world. Political correctness, itself an immobilising form of hysteria, forbids the question, but, for those of us who prefer politically incorrect discourse to politically correct incineration or other forms of complicity in our premature demise, this question must be given voice: just what is it that turns the mantra of a beatific chant of faith, such as *Allah akbar*, into a summons to an orgy of death? Why did Martin Scorsese's *The Last Temptation of Christ* arouse violent reactions, condemnations and exhortations to boycotts, as has more recently Mel Gibson's *The Passion of Christ*, but not a universal outcry for the murder of the cineastes, or of those who dared participate in these interpretative exercises?

The fault, of course, is not in religion, but in the fanatic of every religion. Fanaticism remains the greatest carrier of the spores of fear, and the rhetoric of religion, with the hysteria it so readily generates, is fast becoming the readiest killing device of contemporary times. Even after half a century, films that touch upon the era of Nazi glorification, with their orchestrated chant of *Sieg heil,* continue to send a chill of apprehension down the spines of all with a historical memory. Scenes of mass religious frenzy increasingly resurrect these nightmares, and if Khatami's inspired Dialogue of Civilisations leads, eventually, to the dissociation of the chant of millions to the greatness of God from the gross ultra-nationalist politics lodged in the chant of *Sieg heil,* we will have lifted one corner, a not inconsiderable one, off the shrouds of fear that now envelop life, and humanity.

4

The quest for dignity

The Times newspaper of London, on Saturday 21 February this year, carried the story of the suicide of a teenager in Belfast, Northern Ireland. Apparently, it should have been a double suicide but that youth, after yet another bout of humiliation from his tormentors, decided that he simply could not wait. He was one of a close-knit group of seven, the report continues, who had attended school together and continued to spend all their spare time together. Of the seven, only two still survive. The motor accident that earlier took the lives of three of them may not have been deliberate, but it is on record that one of those three had also once attempted suicide. All lived in fear of some degrading punishment by the local vigilantes known as the INLA. In one case, a fourteen-year-old boy, suspected of being a police informer, was tarred and feathered, dragged through the streets, then 'kneecapped' – that is, shot through the back of the knee, crippling the youth for life. Here is what a consulting psychiatrist in north Belfast had to say:

> In a culture where it is acceptable for a young man to be dragged down an alleyway and shot, children grow up believing there is no such thing as respect for human dignity. They ... often develop anxiety and a fatalistic approach to their own lives.

Now why did the psychiatrist settle on that word 'dignity' over others in his clinical notebook? Why had this youth – as had others – chosen to embrace death rather than live but be publicly tarred and feathered and/or kneecapped, subjected thereafter to cruel taunts by his own-age mates – we learn – who called out, knowing he had been crippled, 'Come out, Barney, come out and play?'

We are trying get to grips with the concept of 'dignity', and why it appears to mean so much to the sentient human, almost right from childhood. Why has it been entrenched in so many social documents across cultures, civilisations and political upheavals? Why was it given such prominence in the Charter that resulted from one of the bloodiest revolutions in human history – the French – and further enshrined in the document for the enthronement of peace after the Second World War, the

Universal Declaration of Human Rights? In one form or the other, the quest for human dignity has proved to be one of the most propulsive elements for wars, civil strife and willing sacrifice. Yet the entitlement to dignity, enshrined among these 'human rights', does not aspire to being the most self-evident, essential need for human survival, such as food, or physical health. Compared to that other candidate for the basic impulse of human existence – self-preservation – it may even be deemed self-indulgent.

Here is another incident from real life, involving, this time, not the individual but the nation, an attempt at breaking out from a walling in, a contesting of the reduction of volition, this time largely of the economic kind. About six years ago, I was approached by a Cuban ambassador to Nigeria, with whom I had developed a warm relationship. He felt that I might know some influential individuals within the United States government or in the intellectual circles that relate to its policy makers. His government, he informed me, was anxious for a resolution of the state of undeclared war between the two nations (these formal and informal probes are part of public knowledge, so I am not revealing any privileged communication). Cuba had weathered the general economic sanctions imposed by the US reasonably well, he said, but after the infamous Torricelli Act, whose provisions extended the ban on trade with Cuba even to her existing foreign partners, threatening them as well with sanctions unless they severed such relationships, that small island began to feel the economic stress of claustrophobia, and sought diplomatic means of breaking the deadlock.

The ambassador said, Cuba is ready to meet and talk with the US on any platform, formal or informal, with no preconditions – oh, except one: *Cuba will not compromise her dignity.* It struck me as a remarkable statement, even then. We are a small people, he declared, we are powerless compared with the United States, but we will not compromise our dignity; we would rather starve to death.

That declaration – *We shall not sacrifice our dignity* – is very much the language of nations, or states, to one another. During conflict negotiations or their aftermath – and I refer here to those unpublicised sessions, familiar to arbitrators – that phrase, an insistent, minimal appeal, surfaces with remarkable constancy, even when all else has been surrendered: let us leave these negotiating chambers with, at the very least, our self-respect. It is very much the historic cry of a defeated people, defeated either through a passage of arms or on the diplomatic field, when they discover that they have no more bargaining chips left. What their representatives are saying is simply: the very least we can live with is an agreement that does not reduce us to slaves of imposition, but makes us partners of consent. Yes, we are compelled to make peace, we submit to *force majeure*, but leave us at least a piece of clothing to cover our nudity. This is the motivation behind every formula of diplomatic contrivance that is sometimes described as face-saving, and wise indeed is the victor who knows that, in order to shield his own rear from the elements, he must not denude his opponents.

Considerations of this intangible bequest, dignity, often remind me of a rhetorical outburst in the United Nations by a Nigerian representative – no, that desperate rhetoric did not lead to hysteria as identified in an earlier lecture, except if one chooses to remark the barely suppressed hysterical laughter in the hallowed halls of the General Assembly. The occasion was the nation's arraignment before the General Assembly on charges of violations of human rights and the denial of democracy under the dictatorship of General Sanni Abacha. In what our apologist must have considered the definitive argument on the subject, he challenged his listeners to combat in more or less the following words:

> What exactly is this democracy, these human rights that we're talking about? Can we *eat* democracy? The government is trying to combat hunger, put food into people's stomachs, and all we hear is democracy, democracy! Human rights! What exactly is this democracy? Does it prevent hunger? Is it something we can put in the mouth and eat like food?

I felt bound to come, quite unnecessarily, to the defence of the United Nations and wrote an article in response, remarking that I had dined in the cafeterias and restaurants of the United Nations on occasion, and had never seen democracy on the menu, nor indeed on any menu in restaurants all over the world. So what, I demanded, was the point of that statement?

Well, while democracy as such may not be on the UN restaurant menu, it is none the less on its catering agenda. So is human dignity. Needless to say, both are inextricably linked. Indeed, human dignity appears to have been on everyone's menu since the development of the most rudimentary society, recognised as such by philosophers who have occupied their minds with the evolution of the social order. Nothing is more fascinating, but permanently contentious, than the kind of binarism attributed to the motoring force of the evolution of this order by Hegel, Nietzsche, Hobbes and Locke among others. The historic man, according to these thinkers, would appear to be a product of a choice between abject submission or bondage, on the one hand, for the sake of self-preservation, and, on the other, a quest for dignity, even if this leads to death. Karl Marx, for his part, felt compelled to distance himself from their deductions, yet even he refused to ignore the importance of that element, human dignity, naming it as a reward that comes naturally with the evolution of man whose labour is ungoverned by necessity. That is the phase when it becomes possible to celebrate *the dignity of labour.* What for us is worth noting today is simply the prodigious output of numerous minds on this theme, nearly all of whom emphasise that the pursuit of dignity is one of the most fundamental defining attributes of human existence.

We could utilise the animal kingdom as our entry point: I have listened sometimes to comparisons of household pets in terms of dignity – a cat, for instance, is usually accounted to be extremely dignified in comparison with a dog. The former is thus regarded because it is aloof, independent and deliberate in its motions while the dog exhibits traits of fawning, dependency and easy excitation. These judgements are of course taken from what human beings have extracted from their own patterns of social conduct. Thus, a predator stalking through the jungle, a 'Tyger! Tyger! burning bright', in those luminous lines of William Blake, is often regarded – especially in the *National Geographic* and by conservationists – as the very epitome of dignity, but watch it when it is devouring its prey or snarling at interlopers and I believe that all thought of dignity is forgotten. I think also that we would all agree that there is not much dignity to be found in the execution of one of those natural functions that even the most exalted, elegant and 'dignified' among us cannot avoid. Or indeed when we are indulging in that activity that guarantees the continuation of the species, but is mostly undertaken simply for the ecstasy of losing ourselves in another being.

Obviously we cannot remain within those parameters of poise, balance, rhythm, control and so on, those attainments that are within the capability or trainability of the animal family, of which our species happens to a be a part – a unique species whose social rituals and conduct have defined it further and further away from the rest of the larger family since the beginning of evolution. Today, we can hardly conceive of the individual outside the membership of a socialised group that constantly reinvents itself; we do not equate ourselves with some static organism under observation in a permanently controlled setting, or indeed with a 'dignified' animal in a zoo. Thus, it is within human relationships that the essence of a human attribute, such as dignity, is most meaningfully sought, not within the self as some mystic endowment, but as a product of social interaction. It is futile to seek out evidence of dignity in the life of an anchorite communing in the wilderness with only birds, reptiles and the elements for company. The essence of dignity that is unique to humanity is manifested through the relations of one human being to another, one human being to the family, clan or community, in the relations between one collectivity and another, however defined, including race relationships.

Regarding this context of relationships, however, one common reductionism that also courts dismissal is that of conduct under suffering. Superficially, acceptance or resignation may appear to convey dignified bearing. Would we, however, place a victim of torture, or of rape, within this category? Definitely, what the very act of violation achieves is to rob the victim of that inherent, individualised, yet social property that answers to the name of dignity. Something is taken away with the act of violation, and that innate entitlement is not restored by one's ability to fulfil social or theological expectations that belong to fortitude. There is no such being as a dignified slave, with or without the tarring and feathering that appears to have been appropriated from the Jim Crow culture of America, for the contemporary humiliation of Irish youths in that territory of unrelenting anomie. When the being that is labelled 'slave' acquires dignity, he has already ceased to be a slave.

The Yoruba have a saying: *Iku ya j'esin lo*. This translates literally as 'Sooner death than indignity'. It is an expression that easily finds equivalents in numerous cultures, and captures the essence of self-worth, the sheer integrity of being that animates the human spirit, and the ascription of equal membership of the human community. This does not in any way belittle other human virtues – integrity, love, tenderness, graciousness, generosity or indeed the spirit of self-sacrifice. Dignity, however, appears to give the most accessible meaning to human self-regarding. Its loss, in many cultures, Japan most famously, makes even death mandatory, exile coming as a second best.

To offer some intimation, at this stage, of our ultimate destination, let us remind ourselves that, as with individuals, so it is with communities and nations. Equally, to identify with a community beyond the self is to take upon oneself the triumphs and humiliations, the glories and mortifications that the larger entity undergoes. The very development and maturation of self-consciousness involves the absorption into one's self of sometimes intersecting rings of community or association – the alma mater, sports clubs, religious societies, the professional register and so on. To non-sporting individuals, or the indifferent, nothing is more absurd than to watch a gaggle of football fans, irrepressible and rambunctious on their way into the stadium to cheer their favourite team, slink out of the same arena like drenched fowl and sink into the pit of depression after their team has not merely lost, but conceded a basket of goals. To remind them at that moment, or even months afterwards, that it was only a game is to court pity or transferred violence for one's failure to empathise with their sense of humiliation. Nothing will serve until their dignity is restored in a victorious rematch. Through a variety of habits, tastes, activities, social interactions, vanities, even hobbies, one acquires, or is inducted into, a new family, an extension of the self that may actually come to take precedence over the immediate family and community into which one is born and where one earns a living. I think of this sense of belonging as Community with a capital C – a community of thought, values and sensibilities, one that, like the quasi-state, transcends boundaries and governments. Often Community is founded on shared historical experience that may be negative – such as political or economic bondage or social marginalisation. Finally, let us not forget, or underestimate, the Community that is religion.

Dignity in the management of Community lies at the heart of our preoccupation. The global climate of fear owes much to the devaluation or denial of dignity in the intersection of Communities, most notably between the stronger and weaker ones, an avoidance of the recognition of this very entitlement, this craving, this inbred addiction if you prefer, in chambers of negotiation, compromises, recitation of statistics and resolutions, including within the United Nations. It is easy enough to speak of, and even condemn, the building of concrete walls that turn whole peoples into prisoners in glorified camps, but somehow the expression of one critical, implicit denial is itself denied: that of dignity. Such a wall reaches beyond its physical terrain, and is experienced as a gesture of disdain against the Community of which such people form a part. If the Berlin Wall was held to reduce the inherent dignity of a people since it circum-scribed their freedom, then a wall in Palestine cannot be viewed with the same regard as is elicited today by the Great Wall of China.

A Community is additionally humiliated through the mortification of its leader, or symbol, never mind what private reservations or criticisms it has of his person, a consideration that has surely contributed to the tendency of the Israeli government, backed in turn by the US government, to top its record of disdain for their 'vassals' with threats to expel an elected leader, Yasser Arafat, from Palestine – that is, after progressively reducing his headquarters to rubble. Let me recall a significant phase in that conflict through an assessment that I wrote at the time, published in *Encarta Africana*. It ended on an image, utilising nearly the exact words, that I borrowed from a now largely forgotten incursion of the brawler Mike Tyson into Great Britain.

After a predictable pulverisation of a non-ranked pugilist, Tyson embarked on his familiar bout of obscenities, but in a language that, even by his standards, shocked his listeners in the lurid portrayal of his demolition plans for his next opponent, Lennox Lewis, for whom he appeared to have conceived a singular hatred. I wrote:

> How … does one interpret the act of bombing Yassar
> Arafat's offices? We appear to have been spared the horror of
> the direct bombing of his residence but, for several
> moments, that insensate outrage did appear to have taken

place – according to one of the early newscasts. Fortunately, it dropped out of the reportage. None the less, confirmation has since followed that a rocket did land within yards of his residential compound, and that the quarters of his bodyguards were demolished. The attacks began even while the UN Secretary-General's envoy, Roed-Larsen, was actually in Mr Arafat's offices ...

The tactics of cutting off electricity, telephones, water, and of course radio transmission around the city of Ramallah, blocking all exits and entrances to and from the city, joined in reinforcing a pugilist's tactics of asphyxiation – working the ring methodically, reducing an opponent to a gradually diminishing space of mobility and oxygen, then zooming in for the kill. Kofi Annan was somewhere around, his intermediary was shuttling between the belligerents. I permitted myself the hope that this United Nations presence would be sufficient to restrain Israel from going any further.

Such optimism was swiftly punished. The gunships returned to the attack and, this time, the assault on the headquarters of Yasser Arafat in Ramallah was followed by further attacks in Gaza. Then the radio station was hit. Then other police training stations, the marine corps, Palestinian Authority buildings, etc. The nerve centres of Arafat's makeshift authority were being systematically destroyed. Barak ... was *tearing out Arafat's heart, liver and tongue – and feeding it to his children, and his children's children*, the heirs of an unremitting hatred that will brand them from infancy and drive the hopes of peace in the Middle East beyond the horizons of generations yet unborn. *[Italicised words courtesy of Mike Tyson.]*

It is becoming impossible to recall a time when death visited this field of incompatibilities in single numbers. Let us bear that in mind as we recall the response of Israel's main backer, the United States, to the escalation of this belligerence, so rooted in disdain that it literally bared an opponent, a beleaguered leader of his people, of all the rags of authority – reverting to our language of conflict bargaining – and left him not a stitch to cover his nudity. Madeleine Albright, then Secretary of State, read a statement on behalf of the US government, but failed to recall the deaths of the Palestinians, failed to share with the world any thought of regret for their deaths, even as she mourned and commiserated with the Israeli government on the deaths of two of its soldiers. Such unstatesmanlike insensitivity, such a crass lacuna in the history of global relationships, which was justly and bitterly seized upon by the Secretary-General of the Arab League, reinforced the glaring question mark on the claims of the United States to be an even-handed partner for peace with the rest of the world.

My mind often returns to that act of global contempt in the Israeli–Palestinian conflict – an attack on the headquarters of Yasser Arafat that began *even while the UN Secretary-General's envoy, Roed-Larsen, was physically in*

Arafat's office! The Secretary-General and his other envoys were also within Palestine – in short, this assault took place right under the nose of the United Nations. If nothing else, that incident must have completed the ongoing erosion of the confidence of a large inter-locking Community – the Arab and the Islamic – in an impartial and authoritative intervention from the world organisation in whom the global community has placed the mechanisms of arbitration. If we have to look for defining moments of despair and desperation within the Community that embraces the Palestinian people, its consciousness of the disdainful dismissal of its worth in international regarding, this surely must rank as one of the foremost – and there have been, alas, uncountable numbers.

~

Dignity is simply another face of freedom, and thus the obverse of power and domination, that axis of human relationship that is equally sustained by fear – its poles doomed to remain in permanent conflict, yet comple-ment each other. I shall expand on an experience that I described in the first of this series – 'A changing mask of fear' – where I commented on the emotional state of my neighbours when we were confronted by a raging fire that threatened to consume our homes, and indeed cast doubts on our very survival if we hesitated a moment too long in its path. I offered a contrast in the feeling of helplessness that one obtains when Nature herself is the force of domination, as opposed to when any human, an equal of others in most ways, takes on the role of dominance or dispenser of life and death, and robs one of the faculty of volition. We need such reminders from time to time to ward off the supercilious cant of those – mostly the purveyors of terror, state or quasi-state, and the vicarious undertakers of human wastage – who wave off human trauma with some profound logic that is presumably embedded in comments such as 'After all, one sudden earthquake or flood kills more people than even a year-long civil conflict in Liberia or Chechnya.' Neither *death* nor *suffering* is at issue.

To return, then, to that California experience: I observed no sense of reduction in self-esteem, no conduct that equated with indignity, despite the fact that we were impotent in face of this assailant. This was Nature at work, impersonal, and with an awesome power that annihilated all that lay before it. The power that is exerted by Nature does not humiliate. Indeed, not even the daily precarious habitation in the shadow of a rumbling volcano such as Mount Etna, which in recent decades sent the inhabitants scurrying yet again for safety, nor the earthquakes that devastated parts of Turkey, and lately Iran – none of these remotely attains the reduction of individual self-worth as does the condition of arbitrary control by another. Those citizens of California who live along the San Andreas fault, that is, live with the consciousness of arbitrary seismic eruption, are unfazed by the possibility of death whenever the earth decides to challenge their rights of occupancy. In the Caribbean, the islanders are inured to hurricanes and the accompanying floods. Mudslides occasionally wipe out ancient habitations and bury thousands, later to be dug up in grotesque shapes of mortality – inhabitants of the Philippines recently joined the ranks of these entombed casualties. None of these victims, however, can be said to exist in fear of humiliation or loss of dignity. Illustrations of the kind of power that reduces our self-worth range from the most mundane, even domestic relationships – such as a tenant's fear of ejection by a landlord in a system that offers neither preventive measures nor legal redress – to a wife or child subjected to constant physical and mental abuse by a husband or parent, an Irish teenager in the grip of terror of a vigilante committee, a Zimbabwean recruit in the burgeoning terror training camps of a Robert Mugabe where some are raped as a mandatory rite of induction.

The nature of power that humbles and humiliates is that which compels the head of a Palestinian family to sit helplessly under Israeli guns, drenched in tears, as he watches his ancestral olive grove, the sole family source of livelihood, fall under the electric saw, tree by tree, to make way for the very wall that will, from then on, reduce his space of volition. Or else wake up suddenly in the middle of the night to find strangers in your bedroom ... a battering-ram has knocked a huge hole in your wall, and a group of armed men are hustling you, your wife and your children into a holding pen – such experiences must rank as the ultimate erosion of one's self-esteem. The diet of the average Palestinian in the Middle East today – for this is where we are headed – the table fare of the average citizen is that forced diet of indignity that even children swallow daily and, worse still, watch their parents undergo; encounters that denigrate their very humanity. The reality of this territory of collective indignity can be studied closely by anyone who can make the pilgrimage – one that is attested as unbearable by United Nations agencies on the ground, by humanitarian groups that are constantly involved and find themselves sometimes at risk – to a zone that is at the very heart of today's climate of fear.

In April 2002, at the invitation of the Palestinian writer Mahmoud Darwish, I formed part of a delegation of the Paris-based International Parliament of Writers – now known as the International Network of Cities of Asylum – that visited both Israel and Palestine. We were there both to convey our solidarity to the imprisoned writers, artists and intellectuals on both sides – imprisoned, that is, by circumstances that defeated even their customary borderless vision – and to bear direct witness to what we saw, what was said and what might be expected.

I shall sum up my apprehension of the Palestinian situation in one word: *humiliation*. No, it was not because of one of our Palestinian guides who kept on repeating, 'We want to live in peace with the Israelis, but let them at least grant us our dignity.' It was not because that word cropped up at least a hundred times – both in street encounters and during the concert of music and poetry that took place in the ancient theatre of Ramallah – as the film made of every step of that journey amply testifies. No, it was simply something that I witnessed myself on this voyage of enquiry, and it affected me so intensely that I could hardly wait to share my disquiet with that Israeli leader for whom I have developed enormous respect after several encounters – Shimon Peres. He kindly received us – the organisation's then President, Russell Banks, and me – in his office, straight from his arrival after a visit to China, while we came in directly from a refugee settlement in the Gaza Strip. Our exchanges were candid, and I said to him, 'What I saw, what I read on the faces of Palestinians, young and old, was *humiliation*. I encountered a people who seemed devoid of a hope for peace, yet desperate for a restoration of their human dignity.'

José Saramago, the Portuguese novelist and Nobel prize-winner, was even more graphic in another encounter, a kind of town meeting that took place in

Ramallah. Indifferent to his popular standing in Israel, he used a metaphor from Nazi concentration camps that continues to ring round European literary and intellectual circles even a full year afterwards. Saramago's intent has been much misunderstood, being considered insensitive and hyperbolic by many, including from within our own rank of literary witnesses, but the very fact that this comparison was wrung out of a friend of the Israeli literary constituency contains its own lesson, and is one that cannot be ignored except at peril.

I witnessed the reality of this humiliation in domestic settings on which the contempt of an occupying force had been visited. I witnessed it at checkpoints. I heard it in the numerous recitations of personal experiences across all classes, in numerous episodes, on the campus of Birzeit university. Most depressing of all, I read it in the eyes of the young, where humiliation had hardened into a resolve *not* to yield up that very ineffable possession, dignity, the loss of which would finally affirm the nullification of their human status. Most frightening of all, I saw it congealed into a hard, cold, unremitting hatred. Yes, I understood the counter-claims of Shimon Peres, his anger at what he read as the treachery of the Palestinian leader Yasser Arafat over that leader's repudiation of a negotiated agreement with former Prime Minister Barak in Camp David. And I acknowledged the weight of responsibility that rests on a leader, whose primary mission must be to shield his people from attacks that have raised the barometer of terror through the relent-less, and undiscriminating, use of the suicide bomber. Nevertheless, it was clear to me that, on his part, this astute Israeli leader, perhaps the most thoughtful of past Israeli leaders, did not truly grasp, or else deeply under-estimated, the factor of humiliation, and the human attachment to that contentious possession – dignity.

The republic of the disillusioned expands by the day. Recruits into its army have abandoned all hope of justice from within and without, but remain committed to one all-consuming pursuit – dignity. As that goal recedes, they come to lose, like the Irish youth, all faith in a universal concept of human dignity and become indif-ferent to the moralities and restraints that hold up the scaffolding of civilised coexistence. These are the willing recruits to the army of terror: the 'harmless neighbour', the shy but pleasant young man or woman who helps with putting out the garbage and wishes you a good morning. Behind that friendly 'Good morning' at a shopping mall, however, may lurk the sardonic smile that is powered by the secret knowledge of a terminal 'Goodbye'.

The quasi-state, we know, sometimes overlaps or interlocks with Community and seeks to take it over. Critical mass occurs at the point at which one can no longer be distinguished from the other, and the overrun Community is seen to appear to bow totally to the control of the quasi-state, if only for a measure of preservation of its own identity. The responsibility that we owe ourselves is to prevent the attainment of that critical mass that then pits one Community against another.

Let us cast aside all further pretence. The genesis of the present climate of fear will be found right within the smouldering heart of the Middle East, that confluence of multiple civilisations within which is nestled the most influential spiritualities of the world – Judaic, Christian and Islamic. The dispersal of the climate of fear therefore rests, fundamentally, in a just solution in the Middle East – it has been said often enough, it cannot be disputed, let no one be in any doubt about it. The time for tergiversations is over, it is time for a holistic confrontation of a global dilemma.

No Community, true, dares succumb to an arrogation of power over the lives of its innocents, and the doctrine of *There are no innocents* must be strategically and morally repudiated. To do less is to surrender our self-esteem, deny ourselves all dignity, diminish our own humanity and indeed forgo our fundamental right to existence. Yet even as we build protective ramparts, and pursue the proponents of that impious catechism *There are no innocents* to the ends of the earth, the mind that aspires to an all-inclusive Community must expand beyond the immediate and address the genesis of the current climate of fear, not as an abstraction, but as a man-engendered reality and, thus, one that remains within the compass of human redress.

Between my first lecture, 'A changing mask of fear', and this, yet another annunciation of posturing power left such a flaming imprint yet again on the world, this time on the railway tracks of Madrid, that there flashed across my mind a moment in the career of European fascism. That was the infamous session in which a General Astrid, in the Spanish Cortes, spat the shout of 'Long live death' in the face of the humanist philosopher Unamuno. That banner of morbidity appears to have been hoisted all over the world. To take it down, the world must act in concert, and with resolve, but must also embrace or intensify a commitment to the principle of justice that ensures that the dispossessed shall enjoy restitution, and the humiliated are restored to dignity.

5

'I am right; you are dead!'

The French nation was lately involved in a contro-
versy over its decision to ban ostentatious symbols of
religious faiths from secondary schools. I was invited
to take part in that debate, and readily accepted. It
was a chance openly to interrogate my long-held
conviction that there should be a period in the development of the young mind when the perception of
differences in humanity is reduced to an absolute
minimum, even if, obviously, it cannot be eliminated
completely. That period, it appears equally obvious, is
that of school pupillage, where the space of instruction is cleansed of manifestations of private wealth,
tastes, class and so on. The symbol, as well as practical

expression of this oneness, the leveller, is of course the school uniform.

Objections surfaced to the mind – the indelicate, even provocative timing of the French government – indelicate to the extent of almost sounding like a declaration of hostilities! Then the positive role of religious symbols as spiritual and ethical reminders in the consciousness of youthful minds at all times, a corrective mechanism when one might be on the verge of misconduct. In short, the mind was readying itself for the dialogue mode, anticipating even its extension into protest demonstrations on the streets of Paris and the wharfs of Marseilles. Capitulation by the government was a possibility. I foresaw a protracted dialogue, from objective to acerbic – the basic philosophy of education, instruction traditions from different cultures, inductions into age-groups in traditional societies, reconsiderations in view of the vastly changed nature of the world since Socrates preached his 'impieties' in the street 'schoolrooms' of Athens …

For some, alas, such dialogue was superfluous. A hitherto unknown group – vying to overtake rivals as the terminal censors of our time – warned the French government that it was next in line for a Madrid-style reprisal, and should prepare for a season of 'sorrow and remorse' for its perceived assault on the Islamic faith. At first I was numbed, then surprised at my reaction. Of course, in the world we now inhabit, it should be only a matter of time before some public target, preferably even a school, is bombed, then the contested Islamic head-scarves would be torn off to serve as tourniquets for severed limbs – and, even, as shrouds.

Here is an even older terminating venture – the iron-ically named 'Right to Life' crusaders in the United States, known plainly as anti-abortion militants. One such group – self-styled the 'Army of God' – boasts a supportive network for its assassins, one that extends to Europe. Their zeal for the conversion of minds requires that they gun down doctors, police guards, and the occa-sional patients or passers-by. Their effective network provided protection for the one who named himself 'Sword of God' while on the run for murder. Another of the same breed of Christian fundamentalists, an ordained priest, was executed in Texas last year, to a chorus of threats by his support group that they would unleash on the American populace reprisals that would make Timothy McVeigh's crusade of vengeance look like child's play. Timothy McVeigh, for the uninitiated, was that remark-able individual who was plagued by a unique social conscience that could be stilled only by his blowing up a public building, one that housed both a state-security department and an infant school. His timing ensured, naturally, that scores of children were blown apart or maimed for life. McVeigh did not profess any religion. None the less, he was a zealot of his own Supreme Purpose, the manifestation of a private irredentism. His chosen grounds of dispute were neither ideological nor theological, but he presents us with a clear psychopathology of the zealot, one who is imbued with a self-righteousness that must be assuaged by a homicidal resolution. It moves all possible discourse away from even the dogmatic monologue of: *I am right, you are wrong* – itself a dead end – to one of: *I am right; you are dead.*

~

The sacred – including the infant crèche – appears to diminish by the day, drowned perhaps by the saturation of the world in the rhetoric of sacrosanctity. Here is another lesson from school, an autobiographical note to consider in the collapse of logical (?) expectations from an evolving world:

The boarding school that I attended in Ibadan, Nigeria, was not without its share of bullies. My class was cursed with a singularly vicious specimen against whom we, the smallest and thus the most vulnerable, adopted a very simple strategy: we formed what, taking our cue from history books, we called the Tripartite Coalition. We summoned the bully into our presence and formally announced to him that, from then on, an attack on any one of the three of us would be considered an attack on all three. We moved together as much as possible, especially when changing classes or on the playing fields. Our strategy held the bully in check for a while but he soon discovered that all he had to do was bide his time – since we could not always be together – and then pounce on the isolated wanderer. Unfortunately for me, I had a tendency to wander off on my own. Because of this, taken together with the fact that he had decided in his mind – perhaps because I was the smallest – that I was the architect of this defence agreement, he constantly stalked me and tried to teach me a lesson.

Well, I also had an answer to that. I schooled myself to keep to a certain perimeter whose centre was the school chapel. I had already developed certain agnostic tendencies – which would later develop into outright atheistic convictions – so it was not that I believed in any kind of divine protection. What mattered was that *he* did. Well, not protection as such, but – interdiction. He could not bring himself to attack me in a house of worship. So I watched him prowl, taunt, dare, and do everything to invite me out to single combat. All he got in return was an equal dose of insults. Then, when the school bell rang for classes, I took off as fast as my short legs could carry me into the safety of classroom.

Even the class bully, a creature of quite indeterminate religious conviction, to the best of my recollection, respected the mandates of *sanctuary*. Today, there are no more sanctuaries left in the world, not even the holy city of Mecca, whose time-honoured serenity was shattered some years ago by a bunch of fanatics. Acting from a most ruthless determination, they destroyed all notion of

113

a peaceful affirmation of faith that eliminated, for a few days of spiritual rapture, all distinctions of race, colour, class, wealth and so on in what sometimes appeared to be a single concourse of *one* humanity. Nothing that the world knows today equals the annual *Hadj* to Mecca, neither the combined pilgrimages of other religions, nor those of rival deities, such as the football World Cup. And thus, appropriately for our times, this proved the setting for the most heinous act of religious desecration that the modern world has known. The recent massacre in Iraq that accounted for nearly two hundred worshippers, a massacre that was timed for the holy festival of the Shiite sect of the Islamic faith, naturally shocks and dispirits, but it counts almost as a footnote to the memory of the outrage that was inflicted on the harmonising potential of that concourse of humanity, one that does have its lessons even for non-Muslims or, indeed, non-believers in any deity.

We have to speak to religion! True, the issue is fanaticism, but this does not exonerate the mother – secular ideology or religious indoctrination – from the lapses of the child. We are obliged to recognise, indeed, to emphasise, the place of injustice, localised or global, as ready manure for the deadly shoots of fanaticism. However, the engines of global violence today are oiled from the deep wells of fanaticism, even though they may be cranked by the calculating hands of politicians or the power-hungry. These sometimes end up being run over by the juggernaut they have set in motion, but the lesson appears to be constantly lost on the next contenders for political domination. They believe that they have uncovered a secret that the erstwhile contender for power failed to grasp, and proceed to unleash a monster on an unprepared polity. It is time for all to recognise that there is no regulating mechanism for the fanatic mind. The sooner this is accepted, the earlier we can move to addressing the phenomenon of fanaticism in its own right. Not for nothing do the Yoruba warn that *sooner than have a monster child meet a shameful death in the marketplace, it is best that the mother strangle it in the secret recesses of the home.* What this means, quite simply, is that the primary burden of exorcising the demon that escaped from the womb rests on the same womb that gave it life. Today, there is urgent need for Mother Religion, of whatever inclination, to come to the rescue of humanity with the benevolent act of infanticide.

It was not theocratic dictatorship, but repressions of a secular order that evoked my sense of unease when, a full generation ago, I delivered a lecture entitled 'Climates of art', to which I made reference at the beginning of this series. There is however a link, unsought, a sense of brutal continuity. That link was the attempted murder of the Egyptian writer Naguib Mahfouz, a Nobel prize winner by the way, but what matters to us is that he was – still is – a writer of his time and, most relevantly, place. Unlike a number of other creative minds trapped within the killing domains of the terminal censors, Mahfouz did survive. So, however, most lamentably, has the poised blade of fanaticism that has become even more proficient and inventive over its agency of execution: the time bomb, the suicide bomb, the sarin sachet and even, possibly, that ominous pod, miniaturised, one that, almost on its own, bore full responsibility for the climate of fear of fifty years before – the atom bomb. Let Mahfouz serve us as a living symbol of that space of creative martyrdom that stretches from antiquity till now, from the communist world of the Soviet Union to Afghanistan of the Taliban through Iran, Ireland, Yugoslavia to North Africa – Algeria most excruciatingly. The space of fanaticism aggressively expands into other nations of traditional tolerance and balance, including my own, Nigeria.

Once, the terminal censor flourished in the arena of ideological insecurity and/or will to total mind domination, where the so-called crime of deviationism – that is, diversion from the strict party line – led, quite simply, to a Siberian wilderness or, straightforwardly, to death. Who can forget the notorious purges and 'show trials' of the Stalinist era! Secular zealotry and intolerance appear to have lost steam, however, although we must be careful not to sing their demise too early. Still, it is largely the religious breed that remains to plague the world, a stubborn strain nestled in the vital organs of humanity from the earliest social orders – as the fate of Socrates eternally reminds us. Now that was one obsessed lover of dialogue, who reminds us that it is from the 'dialectics of the mind' that truth is elicited and tested far more durably than from the monologue. The monologue, alas, continues to dominate the murderous swathe blazed by succeeding religions – Christianity and Islam most notoriously. Deviationism – or heresy – is one short cut to death.

My poem 'Samarkand, and Other Markets I Have Known' was a tribute to Naguib Mahfouz, who was fated to expand into the religious those apprehensions of the secular to which I had given voice in 'Climates of art', delivered some twenty-five years ago:

> ... the ink of Kandahar
>
> *Has turned to blood. The heir of ancient dynasties*
> *Of letters – Khuorassan, Alexandria, Timbuktoo lies sprawled*
> *In the dirt and dust of a passageway*
>
> *He is no alien. No roots than his grow deeper*
> *In that market place, no eye roved closer home.*
> *He is that fixture in the marketplace café*
> *Sipping sweetened cups of mint, oblivious of*
> *The bitter one that would be served*
> *By the shadowy one, the waiter-stalker, a youth*
> *Fed on dreams of sarabands of houris*
> *Doe-eyed virgins, wine and sweetmeats in the afterlife*
> *But to his paradise, a key – the plunging knife.*

117

The nineteenth-century black American scholar W. E. B. Dubois once declared that the issue of the twentieth century would be that of race. It is becoming clear that while that century, the last, did indeed inherit – and still remains plagued near continuously by – that social issue, race was replaced towards the end by religion, and it is something that has yet to be addressed with the same global concern as race once was. The issue of the twenty-first century is clearly that of religion, whose cynical manipulations contribute in no small measure to our current climate of fear. Perhaps the Khatami–UNESCO initiative to which I referred in an earlier lecture, a series of contacts titled Dialogue of Civilisations, will succeed in bringing the world to confront this lethal successor to the secular monologue whose fanatic fringe has been lately deprived of oxygen, and much of its breeding-ground. In the wilds of Thailand or Cambodia, in a few isolated spots in South America, the mind of the fanatic secularist still operates, locked in a vision of Utopia that demands a disposable approach to 'unenlightened' humanity. Pol Pot, however, is dead, gone the way of those other architects of the necropolis, Adolf Hitler, Josef Stalin and mixed company of both left and right. Today, the main source of fanatic mind is religion – and its temper, one that, ironically, is grounded in the doctrine of submission – has grown increasingly contemptuous of humanity, being characterised by arrogance, intolerance and violence, almost as an unconscious vengeful recompense for its apprenticeship within the spiritual principle of submission.

At stake is tolerance, and the place of dissent in social interaction. We would do well, however, to note – for practical ends – the differences between the workings of secular intolerance and those of the theocratic order. Such differences may assist us in assessing the very real threat to human freedom that the closed world of fanaticism poses to humanity. Secular ideology derives its theories from history and the material world. The mind has therefore learnt to pause occasionally and reflect on the processes that link the material world to doctrines that derive from or govern it, to review changes in such a world, test theories against old and new realities – be they economic, cultural, industrial or even environmental. The dynamic totality of the real world is given rational space. Even the craving after comprehensiveness and infallibility – as in the case of Marxism – may result in the exposure of fallacies and inconsistencies or, at the least, ambiguous zones within the theory.

Thus, within a secular dispensation, even under the most rigid totalitarian order, its underpinning ideology – that is, the equivalent of theology – remains open to contestation. Open questioning may be suppressed, open debate may be restricted or prohibited by the state or the party of power, but the functioning of the mind, its capacity for critique – even self-criticism – never ceases. Self-criticism was of course an expression that was much abused under totalitarian orders – Stalinist Soviet Union, China during the Cultural Revolution or Cambodia under Pol Pot's Khmer Rouge. Within those self-righteous regimes, self-criticism meant one thing and one thing only: recantation, and a routine incantation of loyal pledges – according to prescribed formulae – to the party line. Despite those perverted rituals, however, the mind remained a free agent within its own space, free to roam outside the confines of the totalitarian order, to seek, and often find, kindred spirits, and form a conspiracy of non-believers or, at least, sceptics. This factor leads sooner or later to an alternative view, and perhaps to piecemeal erosion of the hermetic system.

Under the theocratic sibling, however, one that derives its authority not from theories that are elicited from the material conditions of society but from the secret spaces of revelation, this disposition of the mind towards alternative concepts or variants is next to impossible. Curiosity succumbs to fear, often masquerading as pious submission. The theocratic order derives its mandate from the unknown. Only a chosen few are privileged to have penetrated the workings of the mind of the unknown, whose constitution – known as the Scriptures – they and they alone can interpret. The fanatic that is born of this dogmatic structure of the ineffable, religion, is the most dangerous being on earth.

Again, it must be conceded that there are, naturally, numerous variants of the fanatic spore – as well as enabling environments. While psychologists and social scientists theorise over cause and effect, the Community is confronted with an immediate choice: either to submit or to protect itself. Poverty is a powerful recruiting agent for the army of the soul, we know that; so is political injustice – but society fools itself if it imagines that these are the only parameters for anticipating, preventing, or responding to a development where the totality of society is indicted to the undiscriminating extent that all are pronounced guilty who do not share this mind-set of the fanatic, or who dare propose a different worldview from that which motivates it. The philosophy that sustained Nazism was not a philosophy for the amelioration of the condition of the poor; on the contrary, it was a philosophy of élitism, a philosophy of the Chosen versus the Rest. And what we must seek is the common denominator that unites the opposite extremes of beliefs and ideologies, but also breeds and nurtures the fanatic, intolerant mind. While we are engaged on that quest, we, the Rest, in whatever aspect of belief we are thus defined, must either submit our necks tamely on this versatile execution block or imaginatively pursue remedial action. This involves, certainly, eradicating those conditions that serve as ready recruitment agencies – poverty, political injustice, and other forms of social alienation – but, even more crucially, demonstrating in an equally determined, structured way, our right, indeed our duty, to implement strategies of self-protection, making it abundantly clear that the other doctrine of the Chosen is intolerable to humanity. To do otherwise is to condone the doctrine that moves so arrogantly from *I am right, you are wrong* to its fatal manifestation as *I am right; you are dead.*

The world would of course be a simpler space to contend with if only religion kept within the domain of the spiritual. Historically, it never has. With the blindly submissive army of enforcers in its midst, ready to be unleashed on profane humanity, the religious is an order that remains incapable of remaining within a private zone that does not translate into *power* – as distinct from *guidance* – over others. There are a few exceptions to this in the world of Religion, and we shall encounter one towards the end. The incursion of religion into the secular domain, appropriating the provinces of ethics, mores and social conduct – and even the sciences – guarantees the clerical dominance of the total field of play. *(What, in the name of all that is unholy, does a council of religious clerics in northern Nigeria know of modern medicine that it commands Muslims to resist inoculation against cerebrospinal meningitis – a scourge in that part of the nation that leaves hundreds of thousands of infants disabled for life – and claim its authority from the Koran!)*

Submission, however, is the very foundation of faith. It is mostly within that theocratic order that we find those extreme offshoots that raise the stakes of those rhetorical devices, already touched upon, to the defining edge of existence. The provenance of faith is the soul and, by extension, the soul's material housing, the body itself. In one easy step, the materialist declaration of *All property is theft* – a theme from one of our earlier lectures – is promoted to one of *All life is theft*. The secular ideologue might be largely content with brooking no dissent through the dictum *I am right, you are wrong,* but the ultimate ambition of the fanatic within the theocratic order is *I am right; you are dead.*

Homicidal hubris is the ultimate hallmark of the fanatic. The ice-pick in the neck of Leon Trotsky, ensconced in the deceptive safety of Mexico, was forged in the same furnace as the knife that sought the throat of Naguib Mahfouz.

~

It is fortunate that we are sometimes able – thanks to modern communication – to identify the intrusion of political opportunism into the workings of religious zealotry, a common enough marriage of convenience that gives birth to monstrosities. And technology – the camera – assists in the close psychological study of mob arousal on religious grounds, such as led to the outrage in India that ended with Hindus razing to the ground an ancient mosque in the state of Uttar Pradesh, on the grounds that this centuries-old mosque had been built on the very spot where Rama, a Hindu deity, first made his appearance on earth. The reverberations of that act have continued to haunt the Indian nation till today, but the immediate repercussions were orgies of killings, including the ambush of railway trains and commuter buses, the virtual 'religious cleansing' of rival, but especially Muslim, neighbourhoods, creating ghost villages and derelict urban sectors.

And here, let us pause, and use this episode to anticipate and silence those who, whenever an outrage that is linked to one religion or another attracts amply deserved rebuke and condemnation, immediately raise alarms of prejudice, sectarian hatred and world conspiracies, tacitly claiming for such structures of faith an immunity from commentary. The world, East and West, including its official organs UNO and UNESCO, was unambiguous in its condemnation of that crime, even as it would later unite in condemnation of the iconoclasm of the Taliban against the historic statues of Buddha in Afghanistan. That former rebuke did not lead to any claims by Hindus that the world nursed a primordial hatred against Hinduism or had entered into a conspiracy to eradicate that religion from the world. What was factually indisputable was more than sufficient: an outrage had been committed, and that outrage deserved to be addressed in its own right, albeit without totally ignoring its antecedents and context.

Similarly, in my part of the world, Nigeria, time and time again, waves of fundamentalist violence have been unleashed on a prostrate populace, resulting in the deaths, often in the most gruesome manner, of hundreds of innocents – men, women, children, without discrimination. The majority of those who have commented – except of course the violators themselves – have been unambiguous in their condemnation of such barbarities committed in the name of religion. They have done so without damning the religion itself, or belittling its precepts. The world cannot, I am certain, have forgotten the massacre that resulted from the attempt to hold a beauty pageant in the capital city of Abuja. The culprits have always earned the names *fanatics, criminals, fundamentalists* and *zealots*. I believe it should be possible to attribute the massacre of innocents anywhere in the world in the same way, thus placing the responsibility for a corrective response on the shoulders of believers and non-believers alike.

On a personal level, I found myself sufficiently exercised to note the Uttar Pradesh event in my poetic calendar of 'Twelve Canticles for the Zealot', published in *Samarkand and Other Markets I Have Known*:

> *A god is nowhere born, yet everywhere*
> *But Rama's sect rejects that fine distinction –*
> *The designated spot is sanctified, not for piety but*
> *For dissolution of yours from mine, politics of hate*
> *And forced exchange – peace for a moment's rapture.*
> *They turn a mosque to rubble, stone by stone,*
> *Condemned usurper of Lord Rama's vanished spot*

Of dreamt epiphany. Now a cairn of stones
Usurps a dream of peace – can they dream peace
In iconoclast Uttar Pradesh?

Few spots in the world today are exempt from the depredations of the fanatic. I believe it should be possible to view the bombing of innocents in the United States, Bali, Casablanca, Madrid or anywhere else in the same way. It is untenable to claim that, because those mass killers themselves implicated, and persist in invoking, the banner of Islam, seeking legitimisation and a killing rapture from that religion, Islam is therefore under indictment. Equally unacceptable is to claim that any condemnation of the act or pursuit of the criminals reveals a hatred of the religion. A world in which a powerful European – and mostly Christian – organisation, NATO, goes to battle against the Christian Serbs on behalf of a battered Muslim population, and brings the head of their violators to justice before an international tribunal, is not a world that is prejudiced against either Islam or Christendom, and the propagators of such doctrines are being not merely disingenuous, but dangerous.

In any case, the Christian world is not one, neither is the Islamic, nor does their combined authority speak to or for the entire world, but the world of the fanatic *is* one and it cuts across all religions, ideologies and vocations. The tributaries that feed the cesspool of fanaticism may ooze from sources separated by history, clime and race, by injustices and numerous privations, but they arrive at the same destination – the zone of unquestioning certitude – sped by a common impetus that licenses each to proclaim itself the pure and unsullied among the polluted. The zealot is one that creates a Supreme Being, or Supreme Purpose, in his or her own image, then carries out the orders of that solipsistic device that commands from within, in lofty alienation from, and utter contempt of, society and community.

The stillborn dogmatism of *I am right, you are wrong* has circled back since the contest of ideologies and once again attained its apotheosis of *I am right; you are dead.* The monologue of unilateralism constantly aspires to the mantle of the Chosen and, of course, further dichotomises the world, inviting us, on pain of consequences, to choose between 'them' and 'us'. We must, in other words, reject the conditions George Bush delivered so explicitly in that ultimatum *'You are either with us and against the terrorists, or you are on the side of the terrorists,'* and in *'We do not require the world's approval since we are divinely guided,'* just as strongly as we repudiate Osama bin Laden's *'The world is now clearly divided into two – the world of the followers of Islam against that of infidels and unbelievers.'* What does this mean for those billions of the world who are determinedly unbelievers? What does it mean for the world of Hindus, Buddhists, the Zoroastrians, the followers of Orisa, and a hundred other faiths that are routinely marginalised in the division of the world between two blood-stained behemoths of faith – the Islamic and the Judaeo-Christian?

We, on the African continent, whose people were decimated, in a time of our own troubled peace, in Kenya and Tanzania, our soil violated by one of the earliest acts of aerial sabotage that scattered human limbs over the earth of Niger, have a special stake in this. The black freedom fighters of southern Sudan, locked in a brutal war of over three decades against an Islamic regime – a genocidal war that has claimed at least a hundred thousand times more lives and overseen a thousand times greater destruction of a people, an environment and a culture than in the Middle East – have not resorted to accusing the Islamic or Arab world of a conspiracy against the black race. They are focused on their quest for liberation from a specified, localised, theocratic and often racist order, against which they have raised charges of an ongoing 'ethnic cleansing' that remains largely ignored by the Western world. It has only belatedly, in very recent times, been acknowledged by the United Nations, through a warning from its Secretary-General, as yet another Rwanda scenario in the making. We do not hear from the leaders of that struggle any proposition of the division of the world into the African world against All Others. The combatants have not moved to set the bazaars and monuments of Medina on fire or burn Japanese infants in their cribs.

Not even the historic – still ongoing in places – denigration of African religions and cultures, or indeed the memory of both European and Arab enslavement of the African peoples, has elicited this inflammatory agenda.

Have we any lessons to offer the world from that same continent of a history of near universal disdain? I can think of one. I dispense it at every opportunity. African religions do not proselytise, but let me break with that tradition yet again in the worthy cause of a global quest for harmonised coexistence, and offer the world a lesson from African spirituality, taken specifically from the religion of the Orisa, the pantheon of faith of the Yoruba people. This religion, one that is still pursued in Brazil and other parts of South America and the Caribbean, has never engaged on any equivalent of the crusade or the jihad in its own cause. The words 'infidel', 'unbeliever', *kafri* are anathema to its scriptures; thus it does not recognise a spiritual division of the world. Despite its reticence, however, it has penetrated the globe and survived in the confident retention by the displaced and dispossessed slaves, its infectious hold extending even to their European violators. Its watchword is *tolerance,* a belief that there are many paths to truth and godhead, and that the world should not be set on fire to prove the supremacy of a belief or the righteousness of a cause.

∾

What we have witnessed in the *ripping out of the heart, liver and tongue* of the United States, the hideous conversion of captive human beings into battering-rams for the destruction of other innocents, is an image of such diabolical horror that the imagination instinctively recoils from its full grasp, even after subsequent, seemingly competitive horrors. It will remain so for years. To accept it as a valid and appropriate response to injustices perpetrated by American governments against other people is to abdicate all capacity for moral revulsion. Those very voices that were raised in condemnation of the violation of a mosque in Jerusalem by an Israeli reservist who massacred dozens of worshippers in cold blood – those are the same voices that are now raised, among others, against the violation of humanity on September 11, 2001. And the passion of those voices must not be belittled, cowed or isolated. And yes, even as the murder of Muslims in East Jerusalem, though it took place in a specific milieu, was a crime against our humane universe, even so must the outrage that was committed on American soil on September 11 be recognised and addressed for what it was – a crime against all of humanity, and one that deserves the sternest collective response of that same Community.

∼

Could the United States have responded differently

immediately after September 11? Perhaps not. Hindsight is a most unreliable judge of such decisions, and those circumstances were clearly unprecedented. Did that nation, however, have to continue along an avoidable path that led remorselessly into Iraq? More specifically, and with no complication of hindsight: why were the weapons inspectors of the United Nations ordered out of Iraq in submission to the will of one nation, *most especially at a moment when Saddam Hussein had openly submitted himself to the authority of that very institution?*

Let us turn to our present dateline. It is still the second millennium, the era of the so-called 'global village'. Concretely, it is the era in which the world has attempted to put in place, after many blunders and derelictions of responsibilities, international courts and tribunals for crimes against humanity. It is an era in which former heads of state are being hauled up for crimes against their own peoples and against others – from Chile to Rwanda. It is the era of the strategy of near-globally upheld sanctions, not always successful, we know, and sometimes excruciating slow in their ability to produce the desired results. It is nevertheless the era of newly reinvigorated possibilities, a new global relevance for the organ called the United Nations. Indeed, perhaps it was stemming from this same consciousness, an attempt to impress upon the world the critical necessity of such an organ in the new millennium, that the Nobel establishment, in its centenary year, chose to honour that organisation, and its Secretary-General, with the Peace prize. We cannot deny or gloss over some of its failures to live up to the world's expectations, to its founding ideas, and to the needs of humanity. We are only too keenly aware of the costly consequences – in global trust, and in human lives – of some of these failures. Nevertheless, we are doomed to despair if we fail also to acknowledge its many achievements, and to accept the fact that it is the only organ in the world that has the authority of legitimate intervention in troubled spots.

Unilateral action, or the appropriation of a global duty of response, by any one nation, serves only to diminish the United Nations. That the greatest culprit in this respect should be one of such powerful achievements as the United States, one that is also host to that organisation, physically, on its own soil, only denotes an enervation of the global vision. That the United States has the capacity for technological, military and economic leadership is not in dispute; what the United States lacks is philosophical leadership, despite its formidable reserves of original thinkers. Adopting a global view of a criminality on its soil, and primarily against its people, the US had the option of placing its formidable capabilities under the moral authority of the United Nations, instilling in her own people the imperatives of a global approach to justice.

AMERICA STRIKES BACK! No, this resort to

what we earlier identified as rhetorical hysteria was not what the world needed to see emblazoning the screens of American television and its international arm, CNN, hour after hour, day after day and week after week as the United States gathered its strength to avenge an acknowledged wrong. Such an orchestration of a people's mood was bound to lead, sooner or later, to the quagmire of Iraq, make the nation lose all ethical mooring in the original cause, embark on an open-ended career of aggressive pursuit that would translate as *America Strikes On – and ON and … On … and On …?* its lethal array of weaponry raised to *awe and shock!*

If certain acts against humanity appear to place their perpetrators beyond dialogue, we must still embrace interrogation – that is, self-interrogation. In what way, in turn, have we contributed to the making of such a moment? Failure thus to examine ourselves limits the long-term effectiveness of response, and brackets us with the mentality of the fanatic who, literally, never seeks to recover, indeed is incapable of recovering, a long since receded moment of doubt, the zone of possible choices, the potential of the routes not taken. That quest is open, universal and ahistorical. For once, the dubious doctrine of *There are no innocents* is grounded in durable matter. Has Marxism triumphed since the killing of Leon Trotsky? What nature of an environment enabled the stabbing of a creative mind, Naguib Mahfouz? Was peaceful coexistence promoted as a result of the demolition of the mosque in Uttar Pradesh? Has the assassination of Sheikh Yassin made the world any safer? What kind of morality of a liberation struggle deceives a fourteen-year-old child into becoming a walking bomb? Does a supposed wall of defence concretise hope or despair across the Middle East – and the world? Why is the woman writer Taslima Nasrin a fugitive from her home in Bangladesh?

Reaching back through time to the thread of my earlier intervention, 'Climates of art', made twenty-five years ago, the last word deserves to be offered on behalf of that last, doubly endangered species (on account of her gender), victim of intolerance and fanaticism, who barely escaped the fate of the Algerian Tahar Djaout and a host of others, standing in for the disdained of the world, seeking equity for all humanity:

> Some words are coarse, obscene, indecent.
> They make a case for censorship, such words as
> Pagan, heathen, infidel, unbeliever, kafiri etc.
> The cleric swears he'll sweep the streets clean
> Of the unclean, armed with Book and Beard. Both
> Turn kindling, but overturn the law of physics.
> For the fire consumes all but the arsonist. He lives
> To preach another day. The promised beast
> Of the Apocalypse left me unbeliever
> Till a rambling cleric apportioned death on CNN –
> Surely that devil's instrument! – on Taslim Nazreen.

She wrote of an equalising God, androgynous,
Who deals, ambidextrous, with the Left and Right.